'It makes my heart skip a beat, my breath comes out in short gasps. "I am Soweto . . . I am a Sowetan." I will always be part of that African community. I do not understand it. I cannot run away.' *Sandile Memela*

'The place helps me to teach him Zulu, Sotho, Tswana, Swazi, Afrikaans, Tsotsitaal . . . because Soweto is a mixed masala, a true reflection of the composition of modern day South African society . . .' *Milton Nkosi*

'I do not like Soweto. I know that it is almost *de rigueur* to sing its praises. But I just don't like the place. I have never written a salute to what may be called its "indomitable spirit", or hailed its "indefatigable diversity", or praised its "boundless courage".' *Michael Holman*

'. . . somehow it's the place you much rather prefer to be. It's magnetic and swallows you up: you become an inseparable part of it.' *Diago Segola*

'When I spent evenings in the Soweto shebeens, I was reminded of London pubs; when I stayed the night, I woke up to the sounds of children playing and dogs barking, which reminded me more of English villages of my youth . . .' *Anthony Sampson*

'. . . you could not have peace without freedom . . . we shouted the "black is beautiful" slogan . . . The student uprisings in 1976 carried us on a wave. Now we were talking about a revolution, a complete overhaul of the political and social system.' *Ruth Bhengu*

'. . . foot it to the townships, specifically Soweto's much-romanticised dusty streets, still the bedrock of urban youth angst. These streets are the midwives of a new, cynical, feisty, rap-inspired Afro-revolutionary vanguard . . .' *Bongani Madondo*

'I was privileged to see the birth of the toyi-toyi. I was witness to the anger of beautiful young people who turned into monsters of death . . .' *Aggrey Klaaste*

Soweto Inside Out

Stories about Africa's famous township

Edited by
Adam Roberts & Joe Thloloe

PENGUIN BOOKS

PENGUIN BOOKS

Published by the Penguin Group
80 Strand, London WC2R 0RL, England
Penguin Putnam Inc, 375 Hudson Street, New York, New York 10014, USA
Penguin Books Australia Ltd, 250 Camberwell Road, Camberwell,
Victoria 3124, Australia
Penguin Books Canada Ltd, 10 Alcorn Avenue, Toronto, Ontario,
Canada M4V 3B2
Penguin Books (NZ) Ltd, Cnr Rosedale and Airborne Roads, Albany,
Auckland, New Zealand
Penguin Books India (P) Ltd, 11 Community Centre, Panchsheel Park,
New Delhi – 110 017, India
Penguin Books (South Africa) (Pty) Ltd, 24 Sturdee Avenue, Rosebank,
Johannesburg 2196, South Africa

Penguin Books (South Africa) (Pty) Ltd, Registered Offices:
24 Sturdee Avenue, Rosebank, Johannesburg 2196, South Africa

First published by Penguin Books (South Africa) (Pty) Ltd 2004
Reprinted 2004

Selection Copyright © Adam Roberts & Joe Thloloe 2004
Introduction © Adam Roberts
Individual contributions © The authors
All rights reserved
The moral right of the authors and editors has been asserted

ISBN 0 143 02459 0

Typeset by CJH Design in 10.5/13 point Charter
Cover picture: Sam Nhlengethwa
Printed and bound by Interpak Books, Pietermaritzburg

*For Ruth
and for the people of Soweto for
their courage and victories along the way*

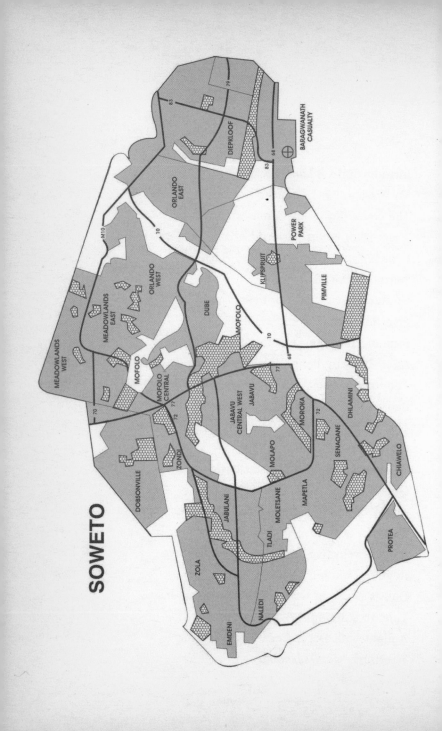

SOWETO

Contents

Introduction

This is a book about Soweto from inside and out. It is an effort to mark a century since the first forced removals of black Africans from central Johannesburg to the banks of the Klipspruit river several kilometres away. It is also in recognition of the limited books available on a world-famous city. A wide variety of writers have contributed: Sowetan experts with views from inside the township as well as interested outsiders who are peering in.

British colonial authorities ran Johannesburg at the start of the twentieth century, as the South African war – the 'Boer War', as the British say – came to an end. They were worried about the effects of overcrowding, poor housing and poverty: they feared disease, but also objected to the idea of people with different skin colours living together. Thousands of gold miners had flocked to the fast-growing city each year from all over the world; unskilled workers were being forced from the South African countryside to provide cheap manpower. A census in 1895 found there were already more than 80 000 people in Johannesburg, up from 3 000 less than a decade

1

earlier.

About half of these were black labourers. But rather than invest in good housing and careful development to cope with the fast expansion, the authorities chose to push the weakest and poorest away. Some were to be dumped on land close to a sewerage works to the south and west of Johannesburg. Those without housing provided by an employer were the main targets. In the part of Johannesburg now known as Newtown (home to the Market Theatre complex) housing for Chinese and black residents was destroyed in 1904. The same year bubonic plague was reported in Johannesburg and 'wretched black inhabitants were resettled in an emergency camp at Klipspruit . . . near the future Soweto' writes one author.

Though the real emergence of Soweto came in later decades, 1904 thus marks the beginning of its existence. In the twenties and thirties as Johannesburg continued to grow, and with it the hostility of some of its white rulers against black people, authorities carried out more forced removals. A 1923 law – the Natives (Urban Areas) Act – obliged local authorities to provide some housing for black people, but also ended their right to own land in most of the city. Barracks were built in the western and eastern townships on Johannesburg's edge. Orlando, the second oldest township within Soweto, was formed in 1931. Its nucleus is on the Klipspruit where people had first settled thirty years earlier. It was named after a councillor, Edwin Orlando Leake, who chaired Johannesburg's Native Affairs Committee.

In 1933 the residential suburbs of Johannesburg were proclaimed as white only and black residents were told to move to townships including Orlando, which by 1936 had a population of about 12 000. Among them was James Sofasonke Mpanza, a political activist, self-declared 'messiah' and a hugely popular ex-gangland boss who, nearly single-handedly, forced the council to provide thousands of extra houses in

2

overcrowded townships. During the Second World War Johannesburg industrialised and sucked in ever-larger numbers of workers to its factories, houses and shops. In the late forties, according to one estimate, as many as 90 000 squatters arrived on the edges of Johannesburg, especially in the area that became Soweto. The government resolved to move remaining black Africans out of many central areas of Johannesburg, such as Sophiatown, to the 'diabolical slums' – in the words of a visiting British writer at the time – on the edges of the city.

Pre-war laws and relocations thus presaged the brute oppression of blacks by whites and forced removals under the post-war apartheid governments. The introduction of apartheid laws formalised a process of black exclusion that had begun much earlier. The Group Areas Act of 1950 divided urban areas into single-race zones and set aside large tracts of good land for the white minority of South Africans. In general, black people were banished to remote and inhospitable homelands, or to townships. A study of forced removals, 'The Surplus People Project', later suggested that three and a half million people were forcibly removed between 1960 and 1983 in South Africa, around half of them bundled out of towns like Johannesburg. Though the city council opposed some of the harsh methods of removal demanded by the national government, by 1955 Sophiatown was being flattened, and many of its tens of thousands of residents were forced to Meadowlands, Soweto.

That broad process meant Soweto was not unique in its formation. There are older townships near Johannesburg, and some of serious political pedigree. Alexandra, cheek-by-jowl with Sandton, is older and has its own share of history to tell. It was home at one time, like Soweto, to Nelson Mandela. Alexandra was also the site of early bus boycotts and protests. Another township, Evaton, also marks its first century in 2004.

In the fifties Evaton had a strong reputation for political activism and bus boycotts. Much further south of Johannesburg than Soweto – it is close to Sharpeville where sixty-nine pro-democracy activists were shot dead in 1960 – its residents fiercely defended their right to own plots of land, despite government efforts to remove it. Many of those who felt unsafe in that township fled instability and sought refuge in Soweto instead.

But Soweto has always generated more interest and attention than other townships. In 1963 Johannesburg's Place Names Commission concluded a four-year public competition with a £10 prize to find an official name for the area, having dealt with a large response. Suggestions included Swestown, Sawesko, Phaphama Villages, Coon's Kraal, Sputnik, Black Birds Bunk, Creamland, KwaMpanza, Khethollo ('segregation'), Oppenheimerville, Darkest Africa and even Partheid Townships. Most insulting were the proposals Verwoerdstad and Hendrik Verwoerdville, after the apartheid leader. But the fact that Soweto was already widely used by residents almost certainly made that name inevitable anyway. It is an acronym for South Western Townships.

Soweto's huge growth came in the post-war decades. One famous resident, Walter Sisulu, believed that the country's modern history is impossible to separate from that of its most famous township. He wrote in 1998: 'The history of South Africa cannot be understood outside the history of Soweto ... The development of the township, and the trials and tribulations of its people are a microcosm of the history of this country. Industrialisation, apartheid policies and the struggle of South African people all find their expression in that place called Soweto.'

But the township only became a focus of world attention in 1976 during bloody repression of student protests, and again during the violence of the eighties. What baffled

4

outsiders, including myself, watching news footage of violence in Soweto is how the South African government deluded itself into thinking it could sustain such misrule. Visitors were equally baffled that ordinary white South Africans could persuade themselves that nothing was wrong. PJ O'Rourke, an American political humorist, describes a trip to Johannesburg in 1988 in his book *Holidays in Hell*. After days with an affable family in a white suburb he concludes that many white South Africans were even trying to deny that black people really existed. He tried to drive to Soweto to meet some: 'A city of two million people and when I looked at my rental car map it wasn't there.' When he finally made it, illegally, he was almost disappointed at how normal Soweto seemed ('most of the houses looked like what you'd see on an American Indian reservation') though delighted by a warm welcome.

That was a time when foreign correspondents based in Johannesburg were likely to go to Soweto on an almost daily basis. Today we are more often found creeping into Zimbabwe than in any of Johannesburg's townships. But if a story requires getting the point of view of 'ordinary people on the street', Soweto is still by far the most common destination for a quick report.

This book is a companion to a collection of journalists' stories about Johannesburg that was published in 2002. *From Jo'burg to Jozi: Stories about Africa's infamous city* was co-edited by Heidi Holland and me. It brought together opinions, prose, poetry, fiction and straight journalism from sixty local and foreign writers with a connection to Johannesburg. I argued in the introduction that Johannesburg is a deeply underrated city. It has a terrible reputation for crime, inequality and

5

hostility. Many outsiders, like me, come to the city for the first time with a sense of trepidation. Some cower in their hotel rooms, so worried about violent crime they dare not go out after dark. But often those who care to look a bit more carefully, and those who spend time in Johannesburg, grow to love the place.

The aim of the previous book was partly to encourage readers to rethink Johannesburg's prospects. Some statistics encourage the idea that the city is improving: apparently crime is declining, at least in the centre of town where security cameras hang on almost every street corner; tourism is growing, from visitors keen to visit game parks and beaches who make a stop in Johannesburg and Soweto en route, but also from Africans who flock to Johannesburg to shop. New developments are encouraging too: there has been a surge of attention given to the Newtown area where restaurants and cafes are opening, now easily reached via the elegant Nelson Mandela Bridge.

Property prices are rising in much of the city, new residential housing and office blocks are going up in Johannesburg. Anecdotal evidence suggests that there is an increasingly hopeful view of the city. I know foreign journalists who have bought houses in Jo'burg in the past two years, and of others who refuse to be posted anywhere else after serving here. Since foreign correspondents are in the business of trying to assess how South Africa is doing, and so are supposed to be informed about the prospects of places like Johannesburg, this is one sign of faith in the city.

I also argued that Johannesburg's future as the capital city of the continent – the Big Guava, equivalent to New York as America's Big Apple – depends on it welcoming Africa to itself. Once Jo'burg was a mining town, a rough frontier settlement. Then it aspired to be a lily-white European city. Many of its white inhabitants were happy to see their black neighbours forced away during apartheid, only to bring them back as

6

day-labourers. Those days should be left behind. To prosper the city needs to become both genuinely African and global, an open and welcoming place, where people of all types mix and work together.

Johanesburg does rank as an international city, as a destination for travellers, a hub for traders, investors, artists and tourists. Its future lies in being a gateway to the rest of Africa too: in the past year two British banks have chosen to set up their African headquarters in Johannesburg; as South African firms spread their business to the rest of the continent, the city is already unrivalled as the heart of continental economic activity. There are long-term plans to bind the Johannesburg securities exchange with stock markets in the rest of Africa. New ports, roads, rail links and overland trade routes are planned from Namibia, Angola, Zambia and other parts of southern Africa to serve Johannesburg. Combined with this growth, the city must welcome more people from beyond its borders. Just as London, New York and Sydney are more vibrant, culturally richer and economically stronger because of the presence of so many migrants, Johannesburg must welcome foreigners. Many of these will come from Africa.

In short, Jo'burg – the white, rather isolated, city of old – must give way to a welcoming, open and mixed city; it could even take up one of the many names that the young and trendy in its midst now use, Jozi. Move from Jo'burg to Jozi, I argued, and be more hopeful about the city's prospects.

From Jo'burg to Jozi included stories from Jozi's townships, from Soweto and Alexandra, as well as from downtown and the northern suburbs. But like many assessments of Johannesburg, it paid too little attention to the big sister city on its south-western edge, a place of some renown but also with a terrible reputation, a place poorly understood but perhaps a bellwether for the rest of South Africa.

7

The aim of this book, therefore, is to look at Soweto. The stories and reflections that follow are written by a hodgepodge of writers from mixed backgrounds, some from Soweto itself, some from other parts of Johannesburg, others from beyond South Africa. This is a book by insiders and outsiders; by local journalists and foreign reporters; by those who are desperately proud of Soweto and those who think it a brash and unpleasant spot. The aim is to provide a collection of pieces from as many different journalistic perspectives as possible: from the expert on the intimate political history of Africa's most famous township, to the roving reporter who can put this emerging city in a global context.

Various themes have emerged in the pieces that the journalists delivered: almost every one an original piece of work written for this book; and each produced, again, in an extremely short time (just a few months from idea to publication). One of the most obvious themes is history: the outstanding reason why Soweto is famous is the part it has played – and continues to play – in the fortunes of South Africa as a whole, as Walter Sisulu noted. Many of the writers give glimpses of Soweto's history through their own experiences there. Ruth Bhengu describes growing up in Soweto, an experience moulded by the restrictions and pressures of the years of struggle against apartheid. Phangisile Mtshali remembers her childhood visits there. Pearl Majola and Nokuthula Mazibuko each describe Soweto through the eyes of their parents; Mongadi Mafata talks to Bomvana, one of the township's oldest residents. Doc Bikitsha's fond memories of reporters – and his descriptions of two other participants in this book, co-editor Joe Thloloe and writer Aggrey Klaaste – bring back to life a time when black journalists worked in strict and discriminatory conditions. Aggrey Klaaste himself gives a broad and authoritative overview of Soweto; while Peter Nkomo offers a straight and honest description of a young man's view of shebeens and 'speakiteasy' drinking days

8

of the seventies and eighties.

One event dominates the history of Soweto and is referred to frequently in the pages that follow. This is the protests of June 16, 1976, when tens of thousands of students defied police by marching against enforced use of Afrikaans in schools. By extension they marched against apartheid as a whole and re-ignited a defiance against misrule that had been shown in Sharpeville years earlier. Their protest, and the brutal suppression of it by police, set in train a course of events that would eventually force the end of apartheid and produce multiparty elections eighteen years later in 1994. After the violence many young South Africans flocked to join the ANC and the PAC abroad. Today many international visitors are drawn to Soweto to see the site of the murder of Hector Petersen, one of the first students to be shot dead on June 16, and the best known because of a world-famous photo. A museum dedicated to the uprising in Orlando complements the excellent Apartheid Museum. Both are obligatory stops on any Soweto tour. But as one contributor, Michael Holman, describes in these pages, even hardened travellers and reporters risk a jolting shock of anxiety when confronted with an ugly past on show.

The writers reach wider than the events of June 1976. Anthony Sampson reviews Soweto life in the fifties when he was editor of *Drum* magazine: Soweto was a friendly haven from Johannesburg; apartheid had the odd consequence of forming a close community among people from very different walks of life in the township. He remembers sitting with Walter Sisulu the day police served a banning order on the ANC leader. Gugulakhe Radebe recalls the demands of police for passbooks in Johannesburg and the humiliating procedures and inspections each applicant had to endure to get a pass. Another writer mentions Kliptown, the site of a different momentous

June event, in 1955, when the Freedom Charter was adopted at a mass meeting. The charter was distilled from contributions by ordinary people all over the country who wanted a free and equal system of government. Many of the wishes expressed in it are also encapsulated within South Africa's widely admired constitution. But persecution of activists who had helped craft the charter led to a Treason Trial of 156 defendants.

Other writers pick up later threads of history. Richard Dowden describes the difficulty of a white foreigner making a clandestine visit to a club in Soweto in the late seventies, though he was not particularly impressed by the music he found. Audrey Brown recalls one afternoon of music and fun destroyed by political violence in the early eighties. Charlene Smith remembers in harrowing detail a violent death at the end of the eighties. Rory Carroll talks to a photographer, Greg Marinovich, who helped to document the killings of this time. By the early nineties political clashes led to especially brutal killings on commuter trains from Soweto, but that eventually gave way to celebrations of freedom and democracy. French journalist Anne Dissez recalls the melancholic end of the partying after 1994, when it dawned on residents of Soweto that some aspects of democracy might be almost as difficult to endure as the old repression, especially as many of the political leaders and the most prosperous businessmen of the township were leaving.

But this is not an attempt to give readers a comprehensive history of Soweto. A few books exist about the township – coffee table photographic portraits are especially popular – and readers will find more detailed chronicles elsewhere. A bibliography listing some books on Soweto is included here. Instead, the pages that follow show slices of life of Soweto, and attempt to place these glimpses into broader reflections or wider debates, as each writer develops his or her thoughts.

As editors we gave few guidelines to the contributors beyond a request, to a wide range of writers, for their experiences and opinions.

One strong debate – and dilemma – concerns the split loyalty of Sowetans who have moved out of the township. As all of the writers in this volume are happy to admit, Soweto is not perfect. This book makes no attempt to romanticise Soweto, a product of apartheid. Eric Miyeni makes a brief but impassioned call to wipe Soweto off the face of the earth. In many respects it is a terrible place in which to live: violence and crime may not be at quite the apocalyptic level that some foreigners and South Africans believe, but they remain very serious. Gangsters still prowl there, as Mark Klusener describes when he relates a late night encounter with 'December'. Rape, burglary, murder, car theft and other crime remain at levels that few would willingly tolerate. Jon Qwelane is not at all impressed with the guns and attacks of Soweto today; he thinks the place just is not lekker any more. Though the murder rate has fallen, recent studies suggest corners of Soweto are as dangerous as anywhere in South Africa. Add the fact that shops and services do not compare with the first-world facilities of Johannesburg's northern suburbs; and count in that Soweto is many kilometres from the workplace of many of its residents. Many Sowetans anyway have strong ties to other parts of Johannesburg. Why then should anyone feel obliged to remain segregated in the dormitory town?

But, despite all this, there is a strong pull to Soweto. John Dludlu finds the warm attraction of a smart new bar in Soweto surprisingly refreshing after Rosebank and the malls of the northern suburbs. Both Milton Nkosi and Sandile Memela write of their anxiety on leaving behind the township of their youth. Both describe lives in the comfortable northern suburbs and yet their uneasy wish to remain as Sowetans, to ensure that their families know the history of the township, that their children learn the accent and languages of its people and become proud of black South African history. There is real anguish in this debate: to move away from Soweto is to leave behind a strong community, to break solidarity with neighbours, school friends and colleagues. Is it wrong to leave, is a question that is implicit in their anxiety. Anne Dissez hints that only those who stayed in Soweto were 'faithful' to their history; but few other writers equate leaving the township with a betrayal of the place.

This debate is reflected in many experiences of the fast-emerging portion of the South African population as it joins a new middle class and leaves behind historic and community roots. It is the experience of members of large, extended families who find they are moving into a world of small, nuclear families. That in turn is a process experienced by people all over the world as working class and predictable lives are exchanged for modern, mobile, middle class, more isolated and individualistic but materially richer ways of living.

The sharply speeded up process for those leaving Soweto in the past ten years should resonate far afield. It is a dilemma about identity: a sense that who you are grows from the place in which you live. Just as some writers anguished in the previous book about leaving Johannesburg for softer living in Cape Town or London, here are ex-residents of Soweto worried about leaving behind their own roots. The title of Sandile Memela's story, 'Tell me, where do you come from?', produces this answer: 'I am Soweto . . . I am from Soweto.' An answer that affirms his identity is bound to irritate some others. Soweto holds such a powerful place in South African history that it often jars for those from other, rougher, townships. Some ex-residents cannot bring themselves to admit that they have left the place behind; they worry they have betrayed a home and a community they love. Some non-residents, including a couple of journalists who frankly refused to write for this book, resent the unfair attention and

12

indulgence they believe Soweto gets. Other outsiders, such as Sam Nhlengethwa whose township collage provides the cover to this book, find Soweto's strength and vitality compelling.

The anxiety that Memela and Nkosi express today is concertinaed by the special history of South Africa – the sudden outflow of its residents would, surely, have been a steady trickle from earlier days if apartheid had allowed it. Other writers take up equally thought-provoking themes, basing their reflections on experiences from Soweto. Anne Hammerstad, a Norwegian, is struck by South Africans' obsessive use of the word 'race' to explain their daily lives. Is everything really about pigment and skin colour even in the new South Africa, she asks. An afternoon in Soweto at Walter Sisulu's funeral provides her with a surprising answer. Christina Stucky describes her arrival from Switzerland a decade ago and the two isolated worlds she finds in Johannesburg's northern suburbs and in Soweto, each existing in an airtight bubble. It is hard to believe that those bubbles are now much less airtight and isolated, ten years on.

But many of the contributions do manage to break away from political history, at least for a time. Several have turned to the daily life of Sowetans. Bongani Madondo finds an emerging youth culture of political, technology-savvy and music-hungry people known as Black Sundayers who gather in Soweto. Mark Gevisser finds life has changed for gay residents of Johannesburg, including Soweto, as South Africa's powerful constitution takes effect. Pearl Majola gives her view of working in Soweto, and how it contrasts with her mother's memories of the place in the fifties. Diago Segola remembers how hard it was to adjust to living in the township after a more comfortable spell in homes in Crown Mines and elsewhere. It was the lack of warm showers in Soweto that hurt the most, he recalls.

One group of stories in these pages, appropriately for sports-obsessed South Africans, tackles the varied efforts to bring sports and games to the township. Marcus Prior, a sports journalist, traces the history of township golf and its more celebrated players. Ofeibea Quist-Arcton uses her Ghanaian-British equestrian savvy to assess a horseriding school, in particular a day when young white riders performed beside black colleagues in the township. James Lamont finds an afternoon watching wrestling in the home of a friend in Soweto a disturbing experience: he worries that the so-called sport projects a skewed image of western culture as violent and brainless, an image that will do Soweto – and the west itself – no good. Keen runner Tim Butcher, who took part in a dawn marathon in Soweto in 2003, concludes it is a tiring but rewarding way to get a view of the place. Nicol Degli Innocenti lingered in a shebeen in Diepkloof, Betty's Joint, whose owner is finally succumbing to demands that she get a big television screen to show the weekend soccer. On his first trip to South Africa, Dominic Hughes spends an evening with the Soweto Rugby Club, while Stephane Mayoux writes of a boxing session with 'Baby Jake' Matlala – four times world junior flyweight champion – at a gym in Dube, Soweto.

The biggest sport of Soweto, football, along with the emerging and popular games of cricket and basketball should have had a bigger place here perhaps. The best of South African soccer also comes from Soweto, as anyone knows who has seen a derby match between Orlando Pirates and Kaizer Chiefs, or who has attended the annual winter football feast in Soweto when the country's best teams compete in a charity match. One of my first experiences in South Africa, a couple of weeks after arriving in the country, was a Saturday afternoon spent watching a series of football matches in Soweto. Going to see live sport, and keeping an eye on those beside you in the stands and seats, is a useful way to gauge the people of a country. I've sat at football matches in Thailand, Argentina,

Ecuador, France, Uganda and Norway and followed teams whose names I can't remember. Though most experiences were more warm and welcoming than an afternoon at an English premier-league game, few places offered the good-natured excitement of my afternoon at the FNB stadium. No one in the huge crowd seemed to care that a foreigner was gawping at their intricately sculpted headgear and asking stupid questions about the names of the players. Instead they passed bottles back and forth, stuck thumbs up when I clambered past them on the seats and cheered and hugged when each of the many goals thundered in.

Though sport is probably the most powerful religion for many South Africans, Soweto is also the right place to get a feel for the more traditional forms of worship. Fred Bridgland traces the dramatic growth of one successful evangelist church in the township over the past decade or so; Sarah Crowe relates the intriguing tale of a black rabbi who said he found his faith in a Nazi prisoner of war camp in Poland and went on to open a synagogue in Soweto. Few tales will top that, but visitors can ask to be shown a bewildering range of religious houses in Soweto, including mosques, that will grow ever more varied given the rich influx of migrants from other parts of Africa.

Those who keep their eyes open will also see other rituals at work, especially at weekends when funerals provide a fair portion of social activity. Heidi Holland reflects on death in the township, and the rituals associated with it. In a time of AIDS, when densely populated and relatively poor corners of urban South Africa are especially vulnerable to the disease, Sowetans find themselves at funerals perhaps more often than any other community in the world. Mfanasibili 'Twoboy' Nkosi is snarled in traffic jams each weekend, caused by ever more funeral processions. More should be done to fight the disease; Darryl Accone describes one small effort, by a French artist, in Kliptown, to raise awareness of HIV and AIDS.

15

Of course even these details of daily life, whether sport, religion, health or music, can be drawn into the heavier realms of history and politics. That was especially true during the days of high tension of apartheid rule. The writers who touch on the music of Soweto – notably Bongani Madondo, Richard Dowden, Audrey Brown – recall that even this must be seen in the sharp and divisive politics of the day. The music of Ladysmith Black Mambazo, the Indestructible Beat of Soweto, Abdullah Ibrahim, Hugh Masekela, Miriam Makeba and of more recent singers, like Vusi Mahlasela and Sibongile Khumalo, is especially powerful because it is music with a purpose: it is driven by anger about injustice, by yearning for political change. When Hugh Masekela sang that he wanted to see Nelson Mandela back home, walking through the streets of Soweto, the power of his music was as evident in the lyrics as in the melody and harmonies of the song.

Finally, a group of the writers put Soweto into an African and international context. Foreign correspondents are often criticised for getting just a shallow experience of the countries we visit. But the other side of the coin is that travelling reporters are able to draw comparisons between the places that they see. My own contribution focuses on a township far from Soweto which I believe sets out how much there is in common between emerging urban areas, even of different centuries. I argue there are reasons to believe Soweto can make itself a much improved place in years to come. Justin Pearce offers another comparison when he describes the slums – and repression – in Angola's capital, Luanda. Simon Robinson notes that Soweto does not only exist in South Africa and reflects on namesake townships he has found during his travels across the continent. He stumbles on a Soweto in Uganda, another in Zambia and a third in Kenya. I have also visited a middle-class suburb of Windhoek, Namibia's capital city, which has adopted Soweto's name. There are no doubt many more of them.

16

This book is a collection of different writing, by a varied group of writers. But it does not try to be exhaustive about Soweto: that would be an impossible task. The previous volume on Johannesburg included some non-journalists, poets, writers of fiction. For this volume we mostly limited the authors to journalists, and so include stories that are more typical of journalism rather than fiction. However, a great variety remains. The number of publications and broadcasters represented in a relatively short book is enormous. Among the South Africans there are writers, or former scribes, from publications as varied as *Drum*, *Sowetan*, *Sunday World*, *Mail & Guardian*, *The Star*, *Sunday Times* as well as the national broadcaster, SABC, and the private and independent channel e.tv.

The international contributors offer an equally varied mix. French press and broadcasters are represented, America's *Time* magazine is here, the respected Africa-news website allAfrica.com is present, a former journalist for Norway's *Dagbladet* is among the writers, as is one for Swiss papers. British media are heavily presented, the *Financial Times*, the *Guardian*, the *Independent*, the *Telegraph*, the *Scotsman* the BBC, and the paper I work on, the *Economist*. In addition, among both the South African and foreign writers there are several freelancers and retired journalists who add to the mix, working for papers such as the the *New York Times*.

Do these writers draw out common threads and opinions? Only in the loosest sense. One basic conclusion I have drawn is that there remains great mystification about Soweto. A barber who cut my hair in Melville in 2001 warned me away from Soweto, assuring me I would be murdered if I set foot

17

there. Many South Africans, black and white, are extremely wary of going near the place – perhaps in the same way that many Frenchmen would avoid the more intimidating banlieues of Paris, or some Britons are nervous of going to Brixton in London.

There even remains great confusion on how many people live in Soweto. Maybe this was deliberate during the days of apartheid, when the white government did not want to admit that a large, permanent urban population of black people would not simply disappear. More recently it might be hard to judge accurately because even a regular census does not account efficiently for illegal immigrants and the homeless. But estimates of Soweto's size range from the most plausible, of about three million people – as suggested by doctors at Chris Hani Baragwanath Hospital for example – to the most ludicrous, of about 600 000. The latter is by the normally reliable Britannica Concise Encyclopedia (2003 edition). A cursory drive through Soweto should convince anyone that this is a city of millions in its own right.

But is it emerging to be more than a dormitory town for the economic giant in Johannesburg? The writers in this book do not offer a simple answer to this. I recently spent time with an owner of a small furniture factory who told me he had worked and lived in Israel, in the United States and in West Africa. A decade ago he chose to return to South Africa and build up a business in Soweto. It has survived, but barely prospered. Too few Sowetans would think of buying furniture in their township, he complained. They go to Johannesburg instead. It is a similar story for other shops and car-sales outlets that appeared in the first years after 1994. Hopes of vigorous business, soaring house prices and investment in new homes soon fizzled: too many rich Sowetans moved to other parts of Johannesburg, and crime remains too high to assure investors that this bit of town is a place to make money, despite its millions of potential customers. Nicole Itano finds a forlorn atmosphere, not unlike a company town that has lost its main industry.

Yet the scene is not unremittingly gloomy. This is a far better organised and developed place than the urban maze of Lagos in Nigeria, the sprawling townships in Congo's Kinshasa, or even the chaotic mess on the edge of Istanbul in Turkey. The monster shantytowns or barrios on the edge of Latin American cities are more intimidating than this corner of Johannesburg. Some tourist guidebooks now recommend that travellers, at least by day, drive themselves in and out of Soweto without having to worry too much. Few guides would be mad enough to encourage tourists to disappear with a hired car into the favelas of São Paulo or into a slum of Nairobi.

Where tourists go, business quickly follows. In one part of Orlando near the former homes of Nelson Mandela and of Archbishop Desmond Tutu (houses of two Nobel prize winners in one small neighbourhood) and beside the Hector Petersen memorial you can find eight bed and breakfast guest houses. Besides stalls of art and souvenirs there are a few restaurants that would not be out of place in the smarter northern suburbs of Johannesburg. Go on the right evening for a meal and a glass of wine and some roads are packed with BMWs and Jeeps, tables are full of beautiful people. Sit in the Nambitha bar, and it seems that Soweto is attracting some real new investment at last. Supermarkets are also rising in each township within Soweto. That symbol of South African development, the shopping mall, is rumoured to be on its way to Diepkloof Extension, a richer suburb within Soweto.

Under pressure to extend their services, more banks are opening branches in Soweto. Cellphone firms already do a roaring trade in the township; some are now testing a new method of paying for goods in Soweto, offering customers the chance to use their cellphones as instant debit cards in some shops. And it may be that more goes on than most people assume. A report in February 2004 suggested that informal trade, spaza shops and street hawkers – usually neglected by economists – actually make up about ten per cent of all retail sales in South Africa. These traders are increasingly important to wholesale suppliers of goods; around a third of them have been operating for at least five years.

None of this suggests that Soweto is about to turn itself into Sandton. But a century after the first people were dumped near a sewerage works on the banks of the Klipspruit, things look much better. If only in comparison to its traumatic and turbulent history, the township today is more hopeful than before. There are enough small indications of improvement – new road signs and maps for Soweto; new shops and bars; investments in sports centres, police stations and community halls; the steady flow of tourist buses – to let Sowetans risk optimism. If Walter Sisulu is right, if the prospects of Soweto and the country are tightly bound together, South Africans as a whole should hope and plan for a happier second century for Soweto.

Adam Roberts
Johannesburg, Jozi
February 2004

My Soweto

Joe Thloloe

Every blade of grass and every stone evokes memories – happy, sad, indifferent. This Soweto is my world, home for sixty-one years, and a microcosm of this country and this continent . . .

Let's drive in from Johannesburg. As you bump into Potchefstroom Road, one of the major entrances to Soweto, you face the Diepkloof Military Camp. Lots of the soldiers behind that gate now come from the township and since our liberation in 1994, our resentment at the presence of soldiers at our doorstep has disappeared.

In the past, the soldiers were mainly white, complemented by black soldiers recruited from the 'homelands'. Our brothers resented us city slickers and seemed to be bent on violence to smother their shame at being soldiers for apartheid. Almost every large township in this country had a military camp at its gate, to help control 'the natives'.

My mind goes even further back, to the time when this

camp was a reformatory for delinquent boys and the principal was Alan Paton, author of *Cry the Beloved Country*. We used to dread the youngsters escaping from the reformatory and committing crimes in the township.

Let's move on. On the right is the youngest of the Soweto townships. It's called Diepkloof and the original residents came in the fifties from Alexandra Township, north of Johannesburg city, and from Sophiatown, west of the city. The land on which Diepkloof now stands was owned by the mining companies and they planted trees after they closed down their mining operations. We'll end our tour back in Diepkloof.

On the left is the Chris Hani Baragwanath Hospital, reputed to be the biggest hospital in the world. Years ago when I was admitted to the hospital for pneumonia it was simply called Bara. I argued with the doctor who admitted me, saying I didn't have to be locked up in a hospital for a minor cold. He insisted.

The following morning, as I lay in my bed, I saw a screen around the bed on my left. There was the smell of death in the ward. A nurse told me that my neighbour had died. A few minutes after they had removed the body, the screen was around the bed opposite me. That smell again.

And then on my right.

In a panic I asked the nurse what had killed the people. She told me all the patients in the ward had pneumonia. Pneumonia!

I don't remember the doctor's name but it's probably thanks to him and the friend who dragged me to the hospital that I'm alive today.

On another occasion, when *tsotsis* carved up my face and reshaped it, it was Bara that helped me back to a normal life. I had fallen and spent all night in the open after *tsotsis* mugged me and hacked my face with an axe. Fortunately it was a bitterly cold night – otherwise I would have bled to death.

When I came to in the ward I went to the toilet. I looked at myself in the mirror and cried. The bastards had smashed the right side of my face in. It took months of operations for the surgeons to reshape my face to what it is today and restore some sight to the right eye. I'm not quite the handsome lad I thought I was then, but this reconstructed pate has served me well.

I do also have pleasant memories of Bara. When we were kids, we would go there on weekends to visit my aunt, who was training to be a nurse. It was fun sitting in the nurses' lounge tickling the keys of the piano. I really thought that I'd one day grow up to be a great pianist. There were also all the beautiful nurses to goggle at . . .

Later, both my sisters became nursing tutors at the hospital. Good memories. But Bara today is schizophrenic. Many doctors around the world would do anything to spend time there, treating that variety of illness and injury they rarely see elsewhere. But other doctors sink into despair when they think of the overcrowding, the long hours and the poor pay.

The irony is that black doctors go into Bara for their housemanship year and then get out quickly to open their surgeries and make money. The white doctors stay for much, much longer, learning and getting out only when they are specialists, with knowledge garnered at this medical gold mine and paradise for researchers.

Bara started out as a military barracks for black soldiers during the Second World War and was turned into the sprawling hospital it is today, after the war.

Opposite the hospital is the bus and taxi rank that feeds people to the city and to all corners of Soweto and the rest of the country. Thousands of minibus taxis and hundreds of Putco buses swallow and spew endless streams of people. And hawkers jostle for space and trade: you can buy anything, from a bottle of expensive whisky to rotting tripe.

Let's proceed to Orlando East, the second oldest part of

23

Soweto after Pimville. On our left is the Lillian Ngoyi Clinic and the St John's Eye Hospital. The eye hospital assisted Bara with the work on my face. The eye surgeons worked on my sight while the Bara ones laboured to rebuild my face.

Turn right, out of Potchefstroom Road, to go into Orlando East. You can't get there without seeing the smokestacks that tower over Soweto. Today they are covered in colourful paint. The intention, I suppose, is to make them look less ugly but I wonder if the huge adverts on them have not introduced a new form of pollution?

Behind that wall is Power Park, a suburb that used to house white city council employees and their families. The gate to the suburb, on Potchefstroom Road, used to be guarded twenty-four hours a day by black council policemen. Under the smokestacks is the Orlando Power Station that once supplied electricity to white Johannesburg. It's no longer in use.

I remember reading Father Trevor Huddleston's *Naught For Your Comfort*. In the book, he related that the power station was one of the biggest in South Africa and that the power lines that supplied electricity to white suburbs ran over homes that didn't have electricity, running water or waterborne sewage.

But this was not altogether true. The houses in Power Park had electricity. So did the house of the township superintendent, our guardian and ruler, who lived here opposite the power station.

In Es'kia Mphahlele's *Down Second Avenue*, he describes how he looked down at Orlando East and Johannesburg city from the stoep of his Orlando West house:

Saturday night. Electric lights! How beautiful they look from a distance. So dull in themselves but, clustered like that, quivering, blinking, little fiery gems set in the fabric of night, they are fascinating. Standing here in a dark little world, viewing them

24

from afar, miles away, you know they are beyond your reach. The more beautiful they look the more distant they appear – or perhaps, the more distant they are the lovelier they look.

Here, a dark township, Orlando; below there, a seething mass of darkness with the usual Saturday night screams and groanings and drums; that's Shanty Town. Up there another part of Orlando with lights, not too far to reach, but smiling and blinking at you ironically; then far away, clusters and clusters of them. They might have been bathed in water and emerged bright, clean, with a crystal texture, in the magical context of night. They look as if you might rake them into a container and leave a sieve on the surface of this summer night. They assume at once the man-made form and the unattainable, at any rate for the moment.

Let's turn right into the first street. On our right, instead of the business premises that are here today, there once was open veld, which for many years was my playground. A few metres to our right, soil erosion had left a deep scar. The older and braver children played hide and seek in its dark nooks.

Easy now, left into Fobo Street and my parents' home. That corner house was a shebeen I patronised occasionally when I was older. A few of the houses in this street were shebeens. That is home.

It's changed a lot from the days when it was only two rooms, a biggish one and a smaller one that was the bedroom. My father started off by dividing the bigger room into two, the kitchen and the living-and-dining-room. And he's been adding other rooms since then. The dining room had small wooden tiles that we polished every Saturday and wiped clean every morning.

I was two days old when my mother came back with me from the maternity hospital in Johannesburg city. She remembers that she used to alight at Doornfontein Station to get to the hospital.

There was a Welcome Dover coal stove in the corner of our kitchen. In winter I loved sitting between the stove and the wall and listening to the adults talking. There were two girls after me and I was boss, except when various aunts and cousins came from the farms to live with us. They were usually older than me and took over the leadership of the Thloloe brats.

My father came from what is now the North West Province and my mother was a city girl from Albert Street in the centre of Johannesburg. She had trained as a teacher in Natal and my father in Pretoria. They started teaching at the Methodist School in Orlando East in 1937, fell in love, married – and then there was me.

We used candles and paraffin lights – right up to the time I matriculated. We carried water from a tap about a hundred yards down the street. I remember the torture of watering the garden – so many trips to the tap, with the heavy watering can slashing my leg. The final straw came when Papa dug into the soil with a garden fork to see if the water had run deep enough. If it hadn't, we had to continue watering.

The toilet was a few yards behind the house. The night soil was collected by men, mainly from Pondoland, who had traditional patterns cut into their faces. When they came at night, using the passage between the rows of houses, they enveloped our homes in a stink. They would open the back cover of the toilet, pull out the smelly bucket and drop the cover with an awful clanging as they emptied the bucket into the tank pulled by their oxen. They used lanterns for light. They'd shout *tshutsha!* – possibly a seMpondo word for 'carry'. We saw them in the flesh around Christmas when they'd do their rounds earlier in the evening. They came into our homes to ask for 'Christmas box'. We would scream and cling to our mothers' legs, scared that they had finally come for us.

What I loved most those years were the books in my home, after all my parents were *tichere* and *mistress*. My father later

26

started a *spaza* shop and it grew into a formal shop at the shelters, *emaplateni*. But wait, I run ahead of my story, the story of my Soweto.

Now you've met my old folk. Still spunky even in their eighties. They still read the newspapers, watch television and argue about politics and Mbeki . . .

Let's go back into the street. The house over there – that's where Boy Gumede lived. Gumede, Texan. Tall, handsome, swaggering in his walk. The first real journalist I met. I admired him. I'd look out for him, listen for the jeep or the Volkswagen that fetched him or dropped him back home after work. I didn't dream that he would one day be my mentor, that I'd sit at his feet as he taught me how to write news stories, drink, really knock back, the brandy. He was a great writer. A simple note from him saying, for example, that you'd find him at Teacher's shebeen at Wemmer Hostel was poetry. He had a way with words.

When I last saw him in New York where he was in exile working for the United Nations radio, I kept goading him to write something substantial, like a novel or a memoir, something by which we'd remember him. He just laughed at me and said he'd do it.

The Texan died in KwaZulu-Natal, Pomoroy, a few months after returning from exile and building his mother a house there. He didn't write that opus.

I loved him.

The houses in this street, as in all those in Orlando East, were either two-roomed, like my home, or three-roomed. This hasn't changed. Many of the residents are now old and have enlarged their houses and allowed tenants to build shacks in their yards to supplement their pensions. In the old days, 'health inspectors' patrolled the township, issuing summonses to anybody who erected an 'illegal' structure. Orlando East was well known for its big yards and colourful gardens. It's now turned into a slum as people crowd in from the rural

27

areas and the hinterland of the continent in search of gold.

Over there is the Lutheran Church. That's where I first went to school – pre-school, they call it today. *Dom A*, they called it then – dumb beginners. All the classes were crammed into the one church hall and we all shouted different things in response to our various teachers.

I carried a mug on my belt and at break we'd queue in the pastor's yard behind the school and collect milk or soup and a slice of brown bread with peanut butter. The schools in the township were run by the churches – Methodist, Anglican, Baptist, Catholic, Presbyterian, you name it.

Over there is the Presbyterian Church, where my grandfather was a minister. He'd originally come from Sweetwaters near Pietermaritzburg in KwaZulu-Natal. He was transferred to Albert Street in Johannesburg and then to this church. He brought his family, with my mother, to Soweto. He retired because of ill-health and lived in Orlando West until his death.

This church is opposite the Plantation, a clump of gum trees that is a landmark in Orlando East. This is where we first saw itinerant evangelists for the first time. Reverend Bhengu of the Assemblies of God came here from Port Elizabeth in the fifties and he would pitch a gigantic tent and conduct revivalist crusades, booming through loudspeakers.

I can't tell the story of Soweto without telling the story of the 'miracles' I saw in that tent. One evening, I saw the shoemaker who occupied the shop next to my father's at the Shelters. He struggled out of his wheelchair and stood on his crutches as Bhengu prayed for him. The shoemaker shouted, threw his crutches aside and said he'd been healed. We shouted, Alleluia, Amen. I was amazed. Hell, I knew the man well.

I lost him in the melee after the service but the next day I peeped into his shop. He was back on his wheelchair. His crutches were beside him. To this day, I can't explain what happened that night or all the nights and afternoons I saw the miracles. One day, one day I might be able to explain it.

28

Down this road is Law Palmer Primary School, right next to Orlando High School, the Rock. My home and these schools shaped who I am today. Law Palmer was a Baptist school and the minister here used to be a guest preacher in Bhengu's tent. I spent six years in this school instead of the normal eight. I got a first class pass and moved over the fence to the Rock. It was the age of dedicated teachers, who were paid very little but taught for the love of their work and their people.

The story of the Rock is the story of Soweto, of our country, of our liberation. It is the story of Nakeni, the first principal when it was founded in 1935, Zeph Mothopeng, Es'kia Mphahlele, Ike Matlare, Khabi Mngoma, Richard Gugushe, TW Kambule, Lawrence Mathabathe, of the struggle against Bantu Education . . .

Irony is that this building you see now is not the original one, not the building where I was educated. That building was stolen brick by brick in the early eighties and used to erect shacks in the backyards of Orlando East houses. When this two-storey building was erected at the end of the eighties, the architects had no feeling for the history of the Rock. As I stand here, I don't feel anything for these bricks. My breast doesn't swell with pride, as the cliché goes.

I do however remember the battles fought on these grounds. When Dr Hendrik Verwoerd introduced the Bantu Education legislation in Parliament in 1953, some of the best teachers at Orlando High protested and were fired by the department. A large number of the students joined them at a private school they started in a hall up the street. The government clamped down on it, made it illegal to open a school outside the system of Bantu Education, and banned the students from attending school for a number of years.

Mothopeng went on to become leader of the Pan Africanist Congress, Es'kia Mphahlele is now a treasured writer and teacher, Ike Matlare became attorney general in Botswana,

Khabi Mngoma became a respected musician and music teacher.

Talking about these great Africans draws me to the theory I have: that some of our tactics in the struggle against Bantu Education pushed forward Verwoerd's grand plan to have blacks remain 'hewers of wood and drawers of water'.

In 1953 we lost some great teachers. When the new syllabus was eventually introduced in 1956, we lost even more. When the system was extended to tertiary institutions in 1959, self-respecting African academics refused to have anything to do with the newly created Bush colleges like Turfloop or the University of the Western Cape. English academics also refused to teach in them. It was the third-rate Afrikaner academics, those who couldn't cut it in their traditional universities like Potchefstroom and Stellenbosch, who went to the black colleges.

The last straw was the mass exodus of teachers from the profession in 1977 in the aftermath of the student uprisings that started the year before. People like Kambule, Fanyana Mazibuko, Lawrence Mathabathe, the Nkondos and others left our schools. Increasingly weaker teachers produced even weaker graduates, who taught even weaker students in a deepening spiral. It will take generations to truly reverse the effects of Bantu Education. Verwoerd couldn't have wished for better results.

Let's walk up this passage to some of the shops where we bought our lunch of *amagwinya*, polony and milk or cold drinks. Except for the people behind the counters, nothing has changed. Pupils still come in here to get fat cakes and *atchaar*, mango pickle.

Over there is the Bantu Methodist Church, also called Donkey because when the founders walked out of the Methodist Church, alleging it was dominated by whites, they had a donkey with them, reminding themselves that Christ had ridden on a donkey as he entered Jerusalem.

A few metres from the Donkey Church is the home of James Sofasonke Mpanza. A fascinating man. He was the subject of the story that earned me my first newspaper byline, in the *Bantu World* in 1961.

At the time he had become a grumpy old man – irascible is probably the word to describe him. I was walking past the Communal Hall one evening when I saw that the lights were on and there was some activity inside. I walked in to find members of the Soweto Advisory Board in a heated debate – Mpanza wanted the board to change itself into an Urban Bantu Council in line with the Nationalist Party's new dispensation for blacks. The councils were a more sophisticated form of the advisory boards, but they still had very little executive power. Mpanza waved sheaves of papers, which he said were the legislation that made the councils possible.

His opponents argued that the council would be another dummy on which blacks were to suck while whites ruled the country. The ANC had decided in 1949 to boycott dummy institutions like advisory boards and the Native Representative Council. Only people who defied the liberation movement were in the boards. They got into them for the stipends and the graft – for example, they took bribes from people who wanted to jump the queue on the housing waiting list. The advisory board members, *iZibonda*, wielded tremendous power among the powerless.

Mpanza's Sofasonke Party, mainly women, who had been heckling the opposition, won the vote. They were singing and dancing and ululating as I ran out of the hall to find a telephone to dictate the story in time for the next day's issue.

Sofasonke is a Zulu word meaning we'll die together. This had been Mpanza's slogan in the mid-forties when he led people demanding homes to a piece of land along the Klipspruit on the western side of the railway line between Orlando East and Orlando West. The protesters planted acres of shacks. The council responded by building rows of breeze block rooms

31

and allocating a room to each family. Rows of public toilets and taps were built after each block of about five or so rows. The residents used whatever material they could lay their hands on to extend their accommodation. The narrow streets became crooked paths through the maze of shacks.

The shanties just below Mlamlankunzi Station were No 2 shelters. Those in the middle, where we now have middle class housing, were No 1 shelters, and those below the Orlando Station, the No 3 shelters.

Papa had a shop in the row at the edge of No 2 shelters. I played along the Klipspruit with the children from the shelters, we pushed wire cars like all boys do and we played football in the sand. I can still remember the stench from the shelters, the constant smell of night soil, the smell that we endured in the evenings when the *tshutsha* came to collect. In the evenings, Papa would count his takings for the day and we got into the car to drive back to the clean air of Orlando East.

The people of Emaplateni, called that because of the flat roofs, loved Mpanza. He had stood up to the white man and had won roofs over their heads for them. They were not worse off than the people of Pimville or Emasakeni in Moroka, who lived in similar squalor. Buxom women would dance in front of Mpanza, sweeping the ground with their long skirts whenever he came visiting.

If Mpanza's story ended there, it would have been limp – not strong enough to be a tragedy or a ballad. But it ends with Harry Oppenheimer, the mining magnate, donating money to the Johannesburg City Council to build houses for the people of Emaplateni and Emasakeni. Four-roomed structures started mushrooming to the south-west and additional suburbs like Mapetla, Naledi, Zola, Moletsane, and others. Families were carted in lorries to their new homes, the real monument to Mpanza.

There's a tower in Central Western Jabavu, the Oppen-

32

heimer Tower, that celebrates his contribution to creating this city of matchbox houses, rows and rows of them. The tower is just an elevation to give a wide view of Soweto, but a monument all the same. The plans for this type of housing were used for black housing throughout the country.

So where to now?

I can take you deeper into Soweto and show you places where the shacks have again blossomed – Kliptown Shanty Town, for example, or into the backyards of Soweto. The clamour for housing didn't die with Mpanza, the old fox. More and more poor people are coming into the township and all they can find are cardboard boxes and corrugated iron and dung to build shelters and hope to get jobs in the city.

Let me instead take you to Diepkloof, past Noordgesig on our left. Noordgesig was a township for 'coloureds'. Their townships were always built as a buffer between whites and us. Go into any town, and you'll find this buffer. Their houses were marginally better than ours: they had four rooms, running water and showers inside. This street was the boundary between Noordgesig and Orlando East, but both sides criss-crossed it. We drank in shebeens and found love on the other side; they came this side and found shebeens and beerhalls and love. Man was bigger than the laws written in parliament.

Diepkloof was a plantation that was cleared to make way for these houses. They first cut the tarred roads and then started building the houses. Before they could bring the people who were moved against their will from Alexandra Township and Sophiatown, Papa would bring me here on Sundays and teach me how to drive. I was fourteen then and barely reached the pedals. It had quiet roads with no people.

Today the older part of Diepkloof is like Orlando East, with crowded shacks and squalor in the backyards. The streets teem with unemployed youngsters. Further up the road, another shanty town and then beyond that, the new Diepkloof with homes that look and feel like the homes in the northern suburbs of Johannesburg.

There was a time not long ago when upward mobility started with a house in Orlando, then a jump to a home in Zone 5 of Pimville, and then, the crown, a home in this part of Diepkloof. Irvin Khoza, boss of Orlando Pirates Football Club, has a home here. Renowned journalists like Aggrey Klaaste and Alf Kumalo, moved in here. So did Winnie Mandela.

Now there is another step added at the top – a home in the northern suburbs. Many now skip the intermediate steps and start in a flat in the northern suburbs. In many ways, life has changed, in others it hasn't. The grime and grind persist. Remember what Es'kia said those many years ago: '. . . They assume at once the man-made form and the unattainable, *at any rate for the moment.*' It's still true today, a century after Soweto was created and a decade after our liberation.

Joe Thloloe was born in Soweto and has been a journalist since 1961 when he joined the *Bantu World*. He has worked for *Post*, *Drum*, *Rand Daily Mail*, *Post Transvaal* and the *Sowetan*. In 1994, after the first democratic elections in this country, he joined the South African Broadcasting Corporation's TV News as Input Editor and was Editor-in-Chief when he left in 1997. He is now Editor-in-Chief at e.tv, South Africa's only private and independent national television broadcast company.

The cover: Kasie art

Sam Nhlengethwa

The time I made the picture on the cover, I was staying in KwaThema, near Springs. This piece was part of a series of works for the Market Theatre gallery that was taking a wide retrospective look at South Africa. It dealt with social and political themes, and the exhibition moved from Johannesburg to Durban.

This piece was inspired by the women traders you see in the townships. You see old women selling vegetables on the corners of the streets, or candies and juice at the gates of the school. There are particular people I've been supporting, women who sell mealies in the township. Like the woman in this picture. Every week a woman would drop mealies off with my family. So, in a way, this series of works was a homage to them. To the women with strong beliefs; the women who are hard workers. This picture is a homage to strong women who maintain their families, who make sure their kids go to school, to widows who keep families together. Once, while in Senegal, my thoughts of such women were enhanced. I watched women moving around the town like ants, selling goods, food and garments. I saw them and was inspired by the women of our own towns and townships. Now I want to support them, through my art.

I am fond of this picture and the show it was in. That show was the one that got me nominated for the Standard Bank Award, which I won in 1994. It was a great honour to be the national artist of the year.

I think that there is something powerful about the environment in the townships: you can feel the movement coming into you, it inspires you. In the morning on your way to work, it moves you. The townships become vibrant on Friday afternoon, after the schools close and after work, at about three o'clock. Where I grew up our house was very close to shops and a beer hall, and we would sit and look at the movement of people. I would be sitting with a group of friends and I'd watch people come by and wonder 'how can I put this onto canvas?' Whether you are in Thembisa, Mamelodi or Soweto you get the very same feeling.

I spend a lot of time in Soweto. My wife is from Soweto; many of my friends and colleagues are from there. On a Friday afternoon, you go into a shebeen, you see guys giving that 'thanks God it's Friday' sigh, then 'sshp', open that beer. It's such a good feeling. I want to do a series on shebeens in different townships. They have so much in common.

Language makes them special. The slang of the township, *tsotsitaal*, that's something I miss if I am away, even for a week. Sometimes I just drive or walk around Soweto, to bring back memories. I love to hear the *neh*, a pause and exclamation in the middle of sentences, it's there. Our language is unique, a concoction of all these tongues, of Italian, English, Afrikaans and more. When we say *howzit* it becomes *ek sê hoesit*. Hi is *heita*, 'where are the guys?' is *was die ouens?*, which is so similar to Afrikaans. Even the word for township, *kasie*, is shortened from the Afrikaans for location, *lokasie*.

We grew up in townships and we learnt how to behave there. I have a stockpile of inspiration from them and my mind is occupied with things that I'm going to do for the next five years, all based in the township. That is a statement on its own. You can go to a township, do your sketches and research and you will get a warm welcome. Townships will always be great: our leaders who are running the country are from these places.

There was trust and unity in townships. In the old days when the government removed people from whites-only areas in cities, people were dumped in the middle of nowhere: look at Soweto and what it was, and what Soweto is today. Houses are homely, some people have beautiful cars and are dressed so fine. There is a unity in the township. When I grew up in KwaThema, I knew each and every person who lived on my street. Families were watchdogs for each other, guarding the houses; there was that bond.

But it broke down: our enemy, the police, came in and broke up that trust. They spread rumours that someone was an informer. Or they came in disguise and petrol-bombed a house. So now we must build our future with another view. This is a different generation.

When I was a child in the township one had respect for the elderly. On a bus you would give up your seat for an elderly person. In the street, if we saw an old man carrying his things from the bus we would help to take his bags to his home, whether we knew him or not. Every elderly person is my parent, that is what we learned. If you wanted to smoke, you had to hide, because any adult would feel ready to say to you 'Smoking? A young boy like you?' As a boy of twelve or so, going to school or to the shop, if you saw a funeral come past, you needed to kneel down and give respect as it went along. It was these small things that made us human. Today

37

youngsters push their own agenda; they do not cherish these things; they will not stand up for older people.

But such places are still rich as a subject of art. There is nothing wrong with the townships. Schools like Orlando High produced the ladies and gentlemen of our country. There are good reasons to be proud of townships: we have icons from there. Soccer teams – in the past the fans of Orlando Pirates were the *tsotsis*, fans of Kaizer Chiefs were 'love and peace boys' – sports in general, athletes, boxers, all these are reasons to be proud of the townships. I'm optimistic that the values of such places will be sustained.

Artist Sam Nhlengethwa says making art, for him, is like riding a bicycle: paint and collage, his two favoured techniques, have become inseparable, like the two pedals on a bike. He now lives in Benoni, but exhibits his work internationally and locally, with recent exhibitions in New York, Cape Town and Johannesburg. He was born in Payneville near Springs, but has lived near Johannesburg since 1993, spending much time in KwaThema and in Soweto.

There shall be art!

Darryl Accone

We round the corner to be confronted by a middle-aged woman carrying an old man in her arms. He lies like a baby against her midriff, but his face is shrivelled and his eyes hold no hope.

A few hundred metres on, the same tableau presents itself. And further on, yet again. Despite repetition the effect is no less powerful, and it becomes easy to understand the impact these beleaguered figures have on the community. Scattered around Kliptown, this image of a woman and a man has got local people talking about a condition that in some circles dare not speak its name. A life-size work of art, replicated and plastered on walls, speaks in simple human terms of how HIV/AIDS is cutting a swathe through the country.

The man, our host explains, is not the woman's father, nor an older relative. He is her husband and he is wasting away. The figures were created by a French artist who had come to

Kliptown at the invitation of the French Institute of South Africa, with a brief requiring only the creation of a work that reflected some aspect of his stay. Without disclosing his professional status, the artist spent weeks playing soccer with residents, drinking in shebeens and eating local delicacies. One day, the convivial visitor slipped out of town for a while, returning later with his delicately rendered couple.

Because of his protracted stay among them, Ernest Pignon-Ernest was not regarded as an arrogant European peddling a pessimistic message about Africa. Rather, his perspective was accorded the respect reserved for an insider and many people in Kliptown said the stark image made them not gloomy but hopeful because it publicly acknowledged the problem.

It was no accident that the artist had come to Kliptown. He had come for the same reasons we are here in an emerging South African democracy. Kliptown is where the Freedom Charter was adopted, at the Congress of the People on June 25 and 26, 1955. Its soaring hopes and ringing declarations of intent, encapsulated in ten injunctions, resonate in the Constitution of the new country that was born in 1994.

And yet, despite its august place in history, Kliptown has languished in a curious neglect since liberation. It is not so much that those glorious days in June have not been commemorated by monuments and formal annual remembrances. It is that many of the residents of Kliptown live as they always did, without domestic running water and sanitation.

As we make our way through the township, the enormity of the problem asserts itself. Every now and then, from a patch of cement, a pipe rises, topped with a tap. We are told there is approximately one tap per twenty households. At less regular intervals, but far more visible, loom blue or green fibreglass structures that more usually serve as temporary toilets on building sites or at large one-off gatherings such as sports matches and concerts. Here, they are the permanent locus of controversy and confrontation and represent a bridge to, rather than a break from, the past.

Years ago Kliptown used the bucket system, as did many townships. Once a week, at night, carts would replace used buckets with empty ones, the whiff of accompanying disinfecting Jeyes Fluid lost in the gaseous wake of their noxious cargo. The advent of portable chemical toilets was deemed an improvement, but as we learn, these are irregularly drained and constitute a health hazard. Worse, the community has divided into those who feel the toilets should be locked and used only by households in their immediate vicinity, and those who believe that they should be open to all.

But there are more points of union than division in the community. There is the universal love for a pair of elderly Chinese shopkeepers whose family have been rooted here for eighty years. I discover, astonishingly, that the old woman behind the counter has no English, only Zulu and Cantonese. She and her husband are rumoured not to have set foot outside Kliptown for half a century. Recently, the couple were robbed at gunpoint and pistol-whipped, an act that enraged and saddened the locals, one of whom assures me it could only have been the work of outsiders.

Another point around which the community coalesces is Soweto Kliptown Youth (SKY), a local non-governmental organisation which runs a library and feeding scheme for school pupils. In the modest library, stocked with reference books, school textbooks and a range of fiction, I am reminded of the eighth section of the Freedom Charter, headed 'The Doors of Learning and of Culture Shall be Opened!'

The reputation of the centre's lunches is so widespread that scarce resources are now deployed to feed dozens of youngsters from nearby neighbourhoods too. No one will be turned away, the young coordinator tells us, recalling the Freedom Charter's 'no one shall go hungry'.

Across town is the old Battery Centre. Inside, we discover people are running a variation on the commercial enterprise

41

that used to operate here. In a back room, rows of car batteries are being recharged. Customers bring spent batteries and take away renewed ones. Running television sets create the most demand, but profits go towards TV's antithesis: music, dance and theatre classes that each week draw dozens of local children to the biggest of the building's rooms.

The government does not give the arts as much care or funding as it should. Nor have they benefited much from private funds. So it is in community initiatives such as this that the future of the arts may lie. That art contributes to community is evident from Pignon-Ernest's work. While Bertolt Brecht asserted that 'Art is not a mirror to reflect reality but a hammer with which to shape it', the Madonna and child-man of Kliptown shows that art can do both.

Darryl Accone was born in 1960 in Pretoria. He has written extensively on film, the arts and culture. His work as a critic and arts editor took him to many theatre, music and dance performances in Soweto. He is the author of *All Under Heaven*, the story of a Chinese family in South Africa.

Growing up in Soweto

Ruth Bhengu

Growing up in Soweto can best be described as a valuable experience. Well, if you don't want to use grim words like 'tough' and 'extremely trying' or downright 'life-threatening'. But it was also exciting, challenging and unforgettable.

One of the first lessons I learned while on the township streets was that if you can't use your fists, you might as well ask your parents to send you to your grandparents in the country. Come to think of it, some parents did send their children to the safety of the extended family in rural areas. But as my parents were townies with no close ties to their ancestral homes, we were stuck in Johannesburg.

In the townships a fight could break out over anything. Somebody could pick a fight with you because they wanted your lunch money or your toys. Perhaps your parents had more money than theirs, or they just did not like the shape of your nose. Fighting skills had nothing to do with gender. I am talking dirty fighting here. Fisticuffs, gouging of eyes, biting, hitting with a brick, anything short of stabbing with a knife or shooting. Guns were a rarity then.

So we learned to look out for ourselves. On summer days the kids from my neighbourhood would form a group, pool their meagre resources and go and spend the day at the swimming pool. There were only two swimming pools in the whole of Soweto. The nearest to us was the one in White City Jabavu, a high crime area populated mostly by pensioners and their grandchildren. The children of White City were fierce. They would pummel you just because your face did not look familiar.

Going to school was a mission. I spent the first six months at junior primary battling layabouts. They would waylay us on the way to school. We had to walk at least ten kilometres to get to school. But I was damned if I was going to give up. Growing up in that environment taught me a few tricks about survival. I can walk without fear in any city no matter how rough. I have a persona that I wear like a cloak. Without saying a word I can tell any would-be mugger to 'stay the hell out of my face'.

Today psychologists would say I had a tough childhood. I think it was enriching. Since we had so little we were forced to be inventive. We made our own toys and created our own games. We knew how to entertain ourselves. There was no television, no fridge, and no telephone. Why, we didn't even have electricity! I still get a little shock when I hear today's kids say they are bored. I mean, they have all these gadgets, computers, TV games, expensive toys, you name it. Yet they are bored and stressed.

We were living under the harsh yoke of apartheid so we had to find ways to make sense of our lives. And we did. We lived life with a vengeance. We had parties, weddings, baptisms, traditional and religious ceremonies. There were rituals to mark births and deaths, childhood and adulthood.

44

We had live bands and community choirs and dance troupes. We had dreams and aspirations way beyond our drab environment. There was a recognisable rhythm to our lives. Young people did not have much in material terms but they had style. They knew all the latest American and European fashions. They were streetwise, which combined with book learning gave them a certain edge.

We had a hunger for learning. We watched movies and read books, from James Hadley Chase to Langston Hughes and Es'kia Mphahlele. We collected comics and records. We made music and wrote poetry. We were interested in world culture. We wanted to know what was happening in the world. Then came the seventies. We were the hippies who espoused love and peace. We listened to underground, rock and country music. The hot favourites were Jimi Hendrix, Rare Earth, Earth Wind and Fire. There was also Bob Dylan, Joan Baez and Joni Mitchell.

By the mid-seventies we had realised that you could not have peace without freedom.

We had been 'conscientised' and we shouted the 'black is beautiful' slogan with conviction. The student uprisings in 1976 carried us on a wave. Now we were talking about a revolution, a complete overhaul of the political and social system. I was working as a reporter on the *World* and was right in the thick of things. They were trying times. Young people were shot, arrested, banned and banished to remote areas. Many had to flee the country. There were funerals and commemorations instead of parties.

For a few years there wasn't even Christmas. But people were still meeting and drinking and dancing and keeping their spirit alive. Shebeens thrived. They were the nerve centre of communities. The most popular among my contemporaries was Irene's in Orlando East. Her two-roomed house would be packed to capacity every weekend. I don't know how she made her money because we did more dancing than drinking since there was only standing room. It took at least thirty minutes to fight your way to get a beer from the fridge. The irony is that when she finally extended her home and there was breathing space her clientele dwindled drastically. We must have loved being squashed like sardines.

A stone's throw from Irene's there was Lee. An icon of the gay community, she was so androgynous, it was pointless trying to figure out if she was a man or a woman. Lee was always surrounded by a bevy of pretty boys. Hers was the one place where homophobia had no room at all.

In Dobsonville there was the very butch Gabisile with a deep gruff voice and a knack for playing the right music. She had a strict dress code and did not take any nonsense from anybody.

The cream of the crop was Rowena's in Rockville. This was where the VIPs drank. These were the doctors, lawyers, businessmen (including upwardly mobile thugs who had suddenly become respectable) and other professionals. Shebeens were illegal and slightly dangerous. You could go out for an innocent drink and end up in a police cell. They also provided space for people to gather and debate social and political issues. There were always heated debates about every subject under the sun.

Some shebeens had interesting names like Falling Leaves in Dube, Fontana in Orlando West and the Airport in Orlando East. Apart from the big and famous ones there was a myriad of small ones run mostly by poor widows. If you wanted to keep a low profile, you could lose yourself in any one of these in any township.

Nowadays people drink in taverns. They are legal so there's no danger. They are also soulless. The most exciting thing for any visitor is watching patrons sit and stare blankly at television screens. The music is often as mind-numbing as the television they compulsively watch. Maybe I am exaggerating. After all I have not lived in Soweto for almost twenty years. All my buddies have moved to the previously white suburbs. So what do I know about Soweto anyway?

Ruth Bhengu has been a journalist for more than twenty years. She has worked for publications in South Africa and abroad including *World*, *Sowetan*, the *Voice*, *Drum* and *Tribute*.

Journos

Doc Bikitsha

Towards the end of the fifties and into the sixties many of the prim and priggish around Jo'burg and the townships were muttering 'what good can come out from this group of journalists?' Excluding myself as narrator, they were talking of the late Stan 'Jimmy' Motjuwadi, the late Moses Casey 'Kid' Motsisi, Joe 'Nong' Thloloe and Aggrey 'Emile Zola' Klaaste.

You'll want to know who they were, where they were from, and why they were there. The last question can best be answered by 'Allah', who, in the lingo of the people or *tsotsitaal*, was the plain, standard Creator, but not the One exclusive to Muslims.

They were working as reporters on the *World* newspaper, which by then had dropped its 'Bantu' prefix. From *Bantu World* to plain, simple *World* was indeed an improvement. The change helped to avoid misconceptions about the word which simply means person or people, like George Bush and

Tony Blair being American and British Bantu. But it had gone derogatory. It was the height of apartheid and its miseries, a time when these journalists thrived on insurgencies of all sorts.

We relied on our own mechanisms to deal with the Nats and their evils, the Group Areas Act, influx control, the Mixed Marriages Act that dealt with 'immorality' issues, prohibition on liquor and the curfew, to mention a few. What these lads did was break all those laws and live according to Allah's grand designs, which were drinking and living normally. I am perturbed at the misconceptions of our drinking habits, or stories that we went on 'suicidal binges'. We never intended to drink ourselves to death. But I would rather leave it to other scribes to describe their longevity with the bottle.

Getting to know each other was not incidental but planned from above, as in heaven, by the Omnipotents. The Batswana aptly call Him 'Ramasedi', the father of light. Stan grew up with me in Madubulaville, Randfontein. He had the man-nerisms of a bantam cock when in his element: proud, arrogant, abrasive. You had to live with him to experience that. Otherwise he was surprisingly good-natured. Casey shared some of these traits but was more subtle. All members of this group were gifted writers and that meant one thing: they read a lot. They were never taught journalism but learnt from proud craftsmen of the job.

Stan behaved like a matador and Casey rode the padded horse, but they displayed a deceiving kow-towing attitude when confronted by the authorities. They hailed each other as 'kid brother'. Stan had more meat on his frame; Casey was sparse. Stan was addicted to sport, golf in particular. He was a caddie, and would be seen swinging away on a parched course in Mohlakeng. Casey wrote about sports well, es-pecially boxing. Both were pub men; Casey had a penchant for statuesque and rather voluptuous women. You'd think his wife was his granny or something. Both decried the fact that they were from 'stupidly large families'.

I met Casey at a teacher-training college in Pretoria. He was editor of the college rag called the *Normalite*. Stan was the assistant editor and nearly all the other positions. After collecting advertising revenues we would refresh ourselves at the nearby slum tenement Marabastad, a well-known assortment of various decrepit structures and abodes. It produced our renowned author Es'kia Mphahlele. We guzzled various concoctions there.

Casey swore me to secrecy on this, as it was a shame to drink *skokiaan* or *sgomfan*. He also swore me to secrecy on the scandalous articles I had written for the *Normalite* under a Muslim pen name, Abdul I think. He was expelled from the college because he refused to identify me as the author of saucy articles in our rag. We reunited on *Drum* magazine, the Lord be praised, and I later met Joe and Aggrey.

Aggrey Klaaste, a child of God-fearing parents, was brought up by hand and went by the name of Emile Zola. That says a lot about his father, who was a disciplinarian, a school master and a senior mine clerk who was known as a *mabalane*, he who writes. To round it off, his elder brother had a lofty name, 'Salisbury', and became a legendary musician and pianist. With that you are able to sum up the boy himself.

I met him in the early sixties when I was the unofficial right-hand man of Can Themba at *Drum* at Samkay House. What I could not believe was young Klaaste's fragile frame and threadbare, oversized blazer from Wits, the university. He looked undernourished.

He was looking for holiday work and as I had just demolished a nip of *mahog*, I was in an expansive mood. I toyed around with him, promising nothing. But when his ravishing sister came to check on him I saw the boy in another light, as a potential bro-in-law. I dashed to Can Themba, assistant editor, singing the boy's praises as an incarnate Norman Mailer or Charles Dickens. I pointed out that his other names were Emile Zola and that he might have the same potential. I never got the sister, but our friendship was sealed.

Young Joe 'Nong' Thloloe was brought along by the late Joe 'Texan' Gumede of Orlando East. This monumental place was called London then. And everything was big about Gumede too. I called him Texan because of his gait and expansiveness. He was also intelligent, worldwise and an exceptional news hound. The Texan was an all-rounder at work, irresistible to the women and his best buddy was Jury Bekuyise Milworth Mfusi, a noted pianist and composer who studied at the African Music and Drama Association at Dorkay House.

How young Thloloe fitted into that scheme of things was a mystery. His African name 'Nong' means bird or buzzard and it fascinated me. He was the very opposite of a menacing, carrion-loving scavenger. For me the mere thought of his bird conjures a deadly-stealthy stare, decay and doom. But Nong had his own stare which told you nothing. Only a slight twist at the one end of his mouth gave away the hint of a smile which did not come. One look at him and I felt like reaching for my hip flask of *mahog*.

But I loved him, maybe because the other three, particularly the 'kid brothers', were always querying my accounting skills as treasurer. Joe was mature beyond his age. I have my personal views of Joe's apparent reticence and nonchalance. Don't forget he was a mere high school lad at Orlando High when he was incarcerated with the Pan Africanist Congress leader Robert S Sobukwe. What do you think a boy learns in that cold cell? Surely it was not about Batman, Superman or Leon Schuster. Thloloe became a young man with the maturity and acumen of an astute adult. I enjoyed him for that and I've never seen a more game lad than him.

His mother, Lily, was strict but tolerated my antics because she learnt about my background and her motherly instincts and intuition took over. The father, Letebele, was sporty enough and knew boys' behaviour. How else could they have accepted my one-to-two-o'clock in the early morning sorties on their home in Orlando East? Even the ghetto fowls were fast asleep!

Staggering, I'd tell Joe's mum, 'I'm on an emergency story, we need your son's expertise, please!'

Cripes! Joe was not even six months on the job. But mummy would say 'keep him safe, he is in your hands and responsibility'. Joe's dad would be grinning knowingly in the background.

Years later when I was recuperating from acute alcoholism in the mental section of a hospital in the North West, the same Nong softly walked into my ward, saying 'Bra Doc, I've come to take you home.'

Four decades later the lads are still with me, except for the 'kid brothers', who must be a right celestial nuisance to whoever is in charge, maybe the big boss Archangel Gabriel. All distinguished themselves as authors and media personalities. The critics would no more ask that question: 'What good can come out of them?'

Sipho Neo Bridgeman Basil Bikitsha likes to be known as Doc or Carcass. He says: 'I was briefed to write about how we journalists lived in the 1950s and 1960s. Hopefully there will be room for that another time. This time I got carried away with some of my characters. But I like this version because I'm long winded. Wish me luck!' He lives in Randfontein and answers the phone by demanding, 'Speak now or forever hold your peace!'

God's sailboat

Fred Bridgland

God. Perhaps that's the key for us writers from other continents who have laboured, not always successfully, to explain what Africa is about to our readers back home. We've used the East-West conflict, black-white tensions, tribal divisions, climatic possibilities, scientific socialism versus neo-liberalism, eccentric psychological studies, crazed dictators, historic imperialism and a dozen other theories as tools to try to unlock the mysteries of Africa.

But not God. Whoever He or She is, foreign correspondents should soon come to understand that He pervades discourse in Africa. In face to face greetings and meetings, in letters of sympathy, in sickness and health, Africans are always thanking God and hoping He blesses you.

In Soweto, God is nowhere more upfront than in a large, modern building whose curved white roofs rise like those of a majestic sailboat above the tiny, apartheid-era matchbox houses of Pimville, the township's oldest and one of the poorest communities.

Some 15 000 Sowetans pack the Pimville sailboat, the Grace Bible Church, every Sunday morning in three successive services. And if in heaven everyone sings, dances, laughs, cheers and hugs like the Grace Bible folk, then I want to be there in that number.

My friend Gordon Goba, known as the Black Prince from his long reign as South Africa's middleweight boxing champion, and his wife Gertie introduced my family and me to the Grace Bible Church in the days when apartheid was still around.

We had met on an exchange programme called *Koinonia* ('fellowship' in Greek), under which Soweto families and those from Johannesburg's privileged suburbs questioned apartheid logic and were paired off with each other in a kind of anti-authoritarian dating game. Our friendship with the Gobas flourished. It has survived both families' different ups, downs and terrible losses, including the shooting dead by police of one of the Gobas' sons, Jabulani.

One Sunday Gordon persuaded us to join his own at the fledgling church. It met in those days in the open air in Rockville, but the young pastor, Mosa Sono, who began with just twenty followers, was attracting thousands to his congregation through sheer dynamism and vitality. Nelson Mandela was barely out of prison and apartheid had yet to die: but our children were cheered and hugged warmly when Sono invited them to stand and wave to the congregants.

Gordon was a bit of a roisterer in his Black Prince days during the 1960s. Still a boxing referee, he takes me to contests where I wince and watch his neatly starched, sky blue referee's shirt turn pink as a fight progresses and as shards of teeth flick out of the ring. But the Black Prince has become Gordon Goba, dedicated family man, mightily supported by Gertie, working to put their fine children through good

54

schools. Gordon's hair has turned snow white since we first met and today he is a church elder, leading prayer meetings and burial ceremonies.

In 2001, after seventeen years in the open air, the Grace Bible Church came in from the elements to its huge, airy, multi-million rand sailboat. Most funds were raised over the years by church members themselves, supported by a secured loan from an insurance company.

I've continued to visit and admire the church and its people. I like to arrive early because for an hour before each service there is the best free entertainment in the whole of Johannesburg. Then the resident hot gospel choir, clad in pastel shirts, backed by guitars, drums, trumpets and electronic piano, rock for God, themselves and the congregation.

As the beat picks up, thousands of behinds sway and waists gyrate in unison. Old mamas, coiffured youths, tots, grey-haired elders and young mums with blanketed babies on their backs sing, dance, clap, whistle and cheer. A bespectacled middle-aged lady, who looks like a school headmistress, begins a conga which is soon snaking among the 5 000. This is fun, and despite my own desperately fragile and very private faith and extreme wariness about evangelism, I can't help thinking Christ would enjoy breaking bread here.

Sono's sermons are also fun. A slim, neatly but not ornately dressed, exuberant man, he has more than a thing or two to teach Thabo Mbeki about connecting with ordinary people. He props his Bible on a glass lectern and moves around the tiered stage, which is adorned only with a small, simple cross. One moment he impersonates a sexy lady walking down a Soweto street, the next he tells his congregants: 'People say to me, "You're a pastor, what do you actually DO? You just spend your whole week waiting for Saturday night when you rehearse what you're going to say on Sunday." '

He does not use notes, but relies instead on an encyclopaedic knowledge of the Old and New Testaments and is constantly referring to precise chapters and verses. His followers carry Bibles and scribble notes energetically throughout the sermon.

He seems to have two messages. One is for the poor, the sick, the suffering: 'Wherever there is pain, wherever there is hurt, we believe Jesus gives us the power to heal the pain of the broken-hearted. We are here to comfort one another at the critical moment.'

He means community solidarity and compassion translated into practical programmes. The church runs support groups for people with HIV/AIDS, for the bereaved and the disabled. It organises counselling for people going through painful divorces and parole programmes for prisoners. 'Let's move away from the mentality of being a spectator,' says Sono. 'We must be players who get involved with issues and persons.'

Nhlanhla Simamane, a 26-year-old in the HIV/AIDS support group, says: 'We try to be relevant, not self-righteous. We take care of people in their homes. We wash them, clean their houses, make sure their environment is hygienic. We also give them emotional support and teach their families how to look after them.'

Pastor Sono's wife, Gege, is also involved in that group. 'HIV people need some super power they can hold on to,' she says. 'We believe that through our workshops and the word of God we can restore people's dignity and moral fibre so that they can be proud of who they are. Our problems, beyond HIV/AIDS, are so vast that sometimes we don't know what to do. Even though apartheid is gone, we still haven't established a community that is at peace with itself.'

Pastor Sono's second message is that people can succeed without waiting for the outside world to provide support. The church runs a computer academy, entrepreneurship, accountancy and literacy classes, a music school, leadership programmes for police sergeants, nursery schools and student support schemes. 'Our children have the right to a better life without crime, violence and abuse,' says Sono. 'We want to equip them to be people of significance in our society, responsible adults who have dreams, careers and world class values.'

In the Grace Bible Church I've sat next to single mothers, failed young gangsters fresh off the streets, people with AIDS and warm grannies who remind me so much of my own bosomy grandmothers. The church also gets support from *buppies* – black yuppies – who arrive in Mercedes and big sports cars beyond my wildest dreams. Sono is hopeful. 'This is a Soweto story. We didn't start a church in a vacuum; we started in a community that is highly spiritual. It's about the people of Soweto and growing a culture of excellence, helping them believe in what they can achieve from the sweat of their own brows.'

That is hard work. As one of his fellow pastors says: 'Even when you open the door of a caged bird, it does not necessarily fly out.' But the Grace Bible Church is getting there.

Fred Bridgland has reported for many organisations from southern Africa, including the *Scotsman*, Reuters, the *Daily Telegraph* and the *Sunday Telegraph* and the Japanese news magazine *Shinchosha* [Foresight]. He has written two books on Angola and another on Winnie Mandela's *Mandela United Football Club*, all of them controversial. He lives in Johannesburg and thinks he may be a Christian, but a very poor one.

Five Roses Bowl

Audrey Brown

It was a Sunday in the early eighties, just before our townships were engulfed in flames and death. I remember that the sky was that special blue that only Johannesburg bestows. It was the day for a festival at the Five Roses Bowl in Mofolo Park, Soweto. It was also the day the struggle got really serious for those of us enjoying our youth, in those years following June 16, 1976.

Here's how it all went down.

We lived in Klipspruit West and Eldorado Park, townships built especially for coloured people, so-called by the National Party but not by ourselves, because we were Steve Biko's children, black and determined to rid ourselves of all the mental and physical burdens of apartheid. We lived right next door to Soweto, and on the days when teargas was being used with vicious liberality by apartheid's security forces against black schoolchildren and workers, we walked around with streaming eyes and burning skin in our nearby townships of Kliptown, Klipspruit, Noordgesig, Western, Coronationville, Eldorado Park and elsewhere.

We did protest against apartheid but not as often, or as boldly, as the children of Soweto. And when we did, we were not shot at as they were, though we got our share of teargas, blank bullets and baton charges. We were at one with them though, us coloured kids, politicised by what we saw and heard, felt and knew. Though absent on weekdays, weekends found us in the various townships that make up Soweto, shebeen-crawling to places called Rowena's and The White House and everything in between. We were young and beautiful and powerful.

We had made apartheid stagger, and we were not afraid. On this day we – my boyfriend, two girlfriends from school and I – asked my father to give us his Audi, again, so we could go and live it up in Soweto. His only admonishment was that we at least put some petrol in the car, and not bring it back empty. So I asked him for money to buy petrol to put in the car, which he gave, but not without grumbling just a little.

This was in the days before hijacking. It was also before jackrolling – a virulent strain of hijacking that flourished in Soweto in the late eighties and early nineties when gangs would hijack people, rape the women and force the men to watch. Being killed was an optional extra, but robbery, rape and torture were guaranteed. This was way, way before all that. But in any case it seemed that we had a much more violent state to contend with, so any harm we visited upon each other paled and was discounted.

We went via another friend's house in Mofolo to park the car. Then we walked to the Bowl where the superstars of the day performed. The band Sakhile was always the headline act: they would be splendidly dressed in white robes and musically sublime under the leadership of saxophonist Khaya

59

Mahlangu and bass guitarist Sipho Gumede. Their seminal song about the events of Soweto 1976, *Isililo*, was always the finale. It still makes me cry with pride at the courage of my kin, and then rage at the men who believed they could silence us with bullets and batons. Ray Phiri and his band may have been on the bill that day, and Sipho Mabuse. These were the top acts of the day, and we were spoilt for choice. We didn't even have to pay to get into the Bowl. It is set in a park with well established trees and beautiful grass, the stage is covered by a snow-white half-dome and is apparently modelled on the Hollywood Rose Bowl in Los Angeles.

Hundreds of people were walking into the park, struggling with cooler bags of alcohol and cold drinks. I don't remember carrying anything. Those who had got there earlier had already started fires, and the unmistakable smell of South Africa having fun – meat on the *braai* – was in the air. The park filled up as we waited for the first band to come on stage.

'One two, one two' rang out as the musicians tested their microphones (we would always joke that they can't count beyond three) and then the music started. I always say that all South Africans can sing – in time and in tune – and I do mean it. We knew all the words of all the songs, and we danced in the sunshine lost in the melody of the band Thetha, waiting for the next band, and the next, to thrill us. Sometimes we would complain that such and such a band should fill out their repertoire, because we knew it so well. We were young and gloriously alive, with very little to fear that Sunday.

And then people started running and shouting on the outskirts of the crowd. I was near the front, dressed to impress in my denim miniskirt and red ballet slippers. High heels don't do well on grass, and if you are getting ready to groove, you have to wear the right shoes. More people started running, scattering among the trees and spilling onto the cobbled streets of Mofolo, one of the older and more gracious-looking townships in Soweto. One of the many things you learn as a child growing up in a township is that when people start running, you follow them and ask questions later. My training later on as a journalist obliterated these instincts: now I run towards whatever it is that people are fleeing.

But this was then. We all started running. My boyfriend held my hand and we raced across the grass, jumping over cooler bags and half tripping on spread-out blankets. I kept asking why we were running. He didn't bother to answer. He had girls in his care, and had to make sure everyone got out intact. I saw people slip and fall on the cobbles and others running between moving cars, all the while shouting that 'they' were throwing stones at us.

We made it back to our friend's house and the Audi, shaken and still mystified. I was confused by the 'they' and the stones. 'They' were usually the police, but police never used stones to stop us. Those were our weapons.

Groups stood around and tried to understand. Eventually we were told that 'they' were activists angered by the frivolity of a music festival while there was a struggle against apartheid to wage. They were calling for a Black Christmas where no one would celebrate anything until apartheid was defeated. Later they came to be known as *comtsotsis*: groups of thugs who terrorised the townships under various guises, often masquerading as activists fighting in the struggle. No one died at the festival, and no one was seriously injured. But on that day the Bowl died. With it died the joy and delight with which I celebrated life in Soweto. I still went there afterwards, to visit shebeens and friends. Later on I went as a journalist to report on violence in the townships. But I never went back to the Five Roses Bowl for an afternoon of joy wrapped in music.

To my knowledge fewer concerts have been held there since: Soweto became known as a place of violence, rather than a place of fun; a place of suffering, rather than one of celebration; a place of struggle only, rather than a striving, living place as well. And by the time we recovered something

61

of ourselves from that vicious, hectic time, things had moved on. We started moving into town – Jo'burg city – and carved new spaces where we would live, love and laugh again.

Audrey Brown is a journalist and broadcaster who lives in Johannesburg. She was born and bred in Kliptown. She still celebrates South African music.

Running through Soweto

Tim Butcher

A white man with a pistol stands next to a road in Soweto watched by a crowd of anxious black faces. They press towards the gunman, weight of numbers inching them forward in spite of his cries to get back. As the tension rises their breathing shortens; eyes flick between the dusty carriageway and the gun.

It goes off but something rather odd happens. Nobody falls to the floor and nobody cries out in agony. This is the start of the 2003 Soweto Marathon.

My day had already begun with a surprise. In pre-dawn gloom by the vast Nasrec sporting complex, I was thrown by an encounter with a man parking beside me. He was on all fours carefully removing the dust caps from the valves on the four wheels of his smart BMW.

'They steal them you know,' he said as I stared. The raise of his eyebrows and the conspiratorial shrug that accompanied his remark were predictable. But what was surprising was the fact that he was black. This man was middle class to his very core: he liked running, was wearing smart designer sport clothes and drove a sharp car. And like any regular, middle-class man in South Africa he was jumpy about crime in Soweto.

So off we went for the race and things got a bit hectic, as those in the middle class like to say. The elite runners, the ones who were contenders for the serious prize money put up by sponsors Old Mutual, the global finance house, crowded the starting line and were squeezed forward by those behind. The starter tried to keep order and half a dozen stewards – teenage girls mostly – tried in vain to push the runners back.

They linked arms and leant against the press, the start time approached and pressure built. For some reason the race was started on a road lined with barbed wire. There was an ugly moment with stewards in danger of being catapulted against the prongs before the race eventually began.

'This is where Africa reminds me of Italy, both the good bits and the bad bits,' said my running partner, a 27-year-old Jo'burg lawyer whose family is from Switzerland. 'There is euphoria, excitement and the sheer free spiritedness but you are never far from chaos and confusion.'

So off we went – more a waddle than a run in my case – along with several thousand other runners clad in vests, shorts and running shoes. It is a myth that all black African road runners prefer to run barefoot. I got to see a lot of black runners as they overtook me that day and I can report that only a few were nude from the ankle down.

Six-thirty am is a good time to get a sense of a community. You get to see it wake up and prepare for another day, a view that is both honest and insightful. In Soweto we ran past big ladies emerging from their homes to dispose of the previous night's dish-washing water. They would hitch up their night clothes and screw up their eyes in disbelief at the sight of the runners streaming past. Their faces silently cried out 'what the hell are you guys, who can clearly afford cars, doing, running around our streets?'

I would be lying if I said there was any display of London Marathon-style crowd mania. I cannot remember more than three people clapping their approval as we plodded round Soweto. But at least the taxi drivers, gathering up fares for the hazardous run to Jo'burg city centre, were polite and did not drive us off the road.

I do remember the smell of thousands of coal fires heating the morning meal. Electricity is an unaffordable luxury for many in Soweto and while you do not notice the smell in the bubble of your motor car, if you are gasping for breath like I was you certainly catch the fumes.

As we ran we saw how Soweto relies on its kerbs. They might be useless ground elsewhere but in the crowded township they are the seat of business empires with unbounded potential.

I saw early-morning barbers cutting hair in salons of nothing but a chair right in the dust next to the carriageway. Customers had to trust their skill completely as there are no mirrors with which to monitor progress. I saw hawkers sitting cross-legged offering up a telephone for public use – not a mobile phone but a regular, desk-top chunky one with a wire snaking off through the dirt. Zulu butchers were hacking to pieces an entire cow that was suspended from a tree, blithely indifferent to health and safety standards.

But my favourite was the ad hoc car workshops that do business in the open. An old exhaust pipe protruding from the ground gives them away. If you want to sort out your exhaust problem, that's where you park and all of a sudden someone with a blowtorch and a set of spanners appears.

The run taught me that those white founding fathers of Soweto carefully picked the site of Johannesburg's biggest township. The location south and west of the city was chosen precisely because it was hilly with valleys in which their black workforce could be concealed. One of the better known parts of Soweto, Diepkloof, meaning deep gorge in Afrikaans, was accurately named by those early urban planners.

As I ploughed up those hills I realised one more thing about those who took on the security forces during the struggle, of those marching for miles and having running battles across wide swathes of Soweto. Those guys, I thought as the blood pounded in my ears, were fit buggers.

Tim Butcher has worked as Africa Correspondent for the *Daily Telegraph* since 2000. As well as Soweto, he has run in a number of unexpected places including the Kruger Park, Sarajevo, Freetown, Belgrade and Basra.

After the Bang-Bang Club

Rory Carroll

Few remember the name, but none who have seen the picture can forget what Lindsaye Tshabalala looked like in his final moments. A human torch, flames peeling off clothes and skin, as another man cleaved a club into his skull.

His sadistic murder is one of the iconic images of Soweto. In the right hand side of the frame a child flees the scene but there is little doubt that Tshabalala is the victim of a collective, mob effort. Black-on-black violence, in the parlance of the day.

It was 1990 and Nelson Mandela had just walked to freedom to negotiate a new South Africa. But in the townships African National Congress supporters and hostel-dwellers of the rival Zulu-based Inkatha Freedom Party were dispatching each other with guns, knives, clubs and petrol.

The conflict's dynamics were complex and partly hidden from outsiders. But the Associated Press picture, published around the world, sent a stark and simple message. Savage

Soweto. It won photographer Greg Marinovich a Pulitzer prize, the Oscar of journalism, and a career chronicling war.

A decade and a half later the township mayhem is a memory, a nightmare period history books put alongside the run-up to the 1994 election and the birth of a peaceful rainbow nation. But Marinovich does not close the chapter so easily. Questions remain unanswered. Why did Tshabalala have to die? What do the killers think today? He also agonises over how the apartheid regime exploited his picture to claim blacks were not ready for power.

The mountains and plains of Ficksburg are deep Afrikaner country. Just four hours from Johannesburg but it feels further. It is here, at the end of a gravel road flanked by cows, that Marinovich, now forty-one years old, lives with his wife Leonie, having more or less swapped wars for anthropological stories which do not require a flak jacket. At a crooked table on the stoep he sips a beer and watches the sun set over a garden of lavender and strawberries.

Wounded four times while covering various conflicts, a foot has nerve damage, a lung is punctured and he has gout. But the photographer is otherwise able-bodied and healthy. If only the same could be said of Soweto. Few perpetrators or victims of the township's atrocities went before Archbishop Desmond Tutu's Truth and Reconciliation Commission, he says, so trauma was left buried. 'Things today are a million times better in terms of avoiding the prospect of a violent death but a lot of hurt and pain from the early nineties hasn't been dealt with.'

You get the impression Marinovich could also have done with a session with Desmond Tutu. 'I went through depression for a long time.' He now seeks explanations from the killers he chronicled. 'Maybe it's because I'm so intellectually and psychologically shallow that I want them to tell me what actually happened.'

Of all the deaths it is Tshabalala's, a hapless Zulu man

68

who stepped off a train at Jabulani station into the arms of an ANC mob, that most bothers the photographer. The man who led the killers was composed, taking his turn to stab with a bowie knife before being handed matches by a youth who had emptied a Molotov cocktail over the victim.

Marinovich only knew the leader as 'the man in the white shirt', but that was enough for a friend with good Soweto contacts to track down the killer and arrange a meeting. The photographer is bracing himself for what some psychologists would call closure. 'I'd like to have discussions about how they viewed what I witnessed them doing. How they feel about it, then and now.'

The other unfinished business is political. Marinovich and his colleagues made their reputations feeding the world images of blacks murdering blacks. They suspected the apartheid regime was secretly fomenting the violence to destabilise the ANC and to instil dread of black rule. But they never managed to photograph apartheid agents arming Inkatha or police instigating massacres. Worse, captions written for the atrocities they did capture often reinforced apartheid propaganda that atavistic tribal rivalry was the cause.

Years later the Truth and Reconciliation Commission established the fact of the state's complicity, but in a way it was too late. Who looks at Lindsaye Tshabalala's fiery end and thinks of cabinet meetings in Pretoria? Nelson Mandela, questioned in 1990 about the picture, said the photographer's motives had to be questioned. For a white liberal South African such as Marinovich it is a sour side to a career high. 'I have more faith in black people than white people,' he says, lest there be doubt about his politics.

His regret is not photographs taken but those that were not, such as white policemen with blacked-up faces. He is considering an exhibition but frets at the ambiguity of his township war images. 'You need 40 000 words to explain just three photographs.'

69

Marinovich and a colleague, Joao Silva, set the record straight by writing a book, *The Bang-Bang Club*, *Snapshots from a Hidden War*, putting in context their pictures and the deaths of two photographer friends who comprised half the club. Ken Oosterbroek was caught in crossfire at Thokoza township outside Johannesburg. Kevin Carter committed suicide. A film of the book is being planned.

Silva, thirty-seven, still covers wars in Afghanistan, Iraq, wherever, but feels scarred by his Soweto days. 'It's very seldom worth it. The emotions linger a lot longer than the impact of the images. I still think about all those people whose lives I intruded upon and the dead I captured with the camera.' Does he wish he did things differently? 'Sure. I should have listened to my parents and become a lawyer or accountant.'

What *The Bang-Bang Club* recorded in Soweto and other townships is a benchmark of how far South Africa has journeyed. The violence was feared to be a prelude to full-scale civil war. It never happened. The rainbow nation has enjoyed a decade of peace, democracy and stability.

When Marinovich revisits Soweto today he finds the bullet holes plastered over but otherwise little improvement in the lives of the poor and unemployed. For the characters in his tableaux of suffering he had hoped for more. He grants himself one consolation. 'At least these things didn't happen in the dark.'

Rory Carroll has been the *Guardian*'s Africa correspondent since October 2002. He travels widely but always looks forward to returning home to Johannesburg. Before Africa he was the *Guardian*'s southern Europe correspondent, based in Rome. He is from Dublin and started out working for the *Irish News* in Belfast, Northern Ireland.

The fabled rabbi

Sarah Crowe

It was a tall story which I only half believed. But even if read with a large grain of salt to hand, it made a great tale. So, after persuading my sceptical, Jewish, editor to take the story, photographer Walter Dladla and I went in search of Soweto's fabled rabbi. He was becoming something of a township legend with facts blurred and missing; but it was a story begging to be told.

It was a Soweto spring in 1983, warm with red dust and the smell of an afternoon thunderstorm hanging in the air. We drove the streets of Dube, stopping now and then to ask if anyone knew where the rabbi lived. Finally we spotted it, unassuming and without a number, a facebrick matchbox house just like all the others, except for one thing.

In the postage stamp garden of his home was a head-high pile of foliage in the shape of a hut. To an Irish Catholic like me that was just an oddity, until I stepped through the front door of the house and into an utterly biblical scene. The rabbi's disciple led me to a front room swathed in greenery. Palm leaves were magically attached to walls and the ceiling. Robust tables were laden with grapes, apples, wheat, tomatoes and oranges. On top of a gold-edged cloth depicting the Star of David was a shofar, a ceremonial horn, and a menorah, a Jewish candlestick. On a wall to the side, though they rather spoiled the effect, were tourist posters of Israel.

There, in the dimly lit room knelt a 55-year-old black African man, yarmulke on his head, draped in a prayer shawl and chanting from the Torah in what sounded distinctly like Hebrew. This was Rabbi Simcha Vuyisile Yoshuah Msitshana.

He explained it was the time of Sukkot, the Jewish feast of the Tabernacles, held at harvest time in the Hebrew month of Tishri. But if you happen to be a rabbi in Soweto in the southern hemisphere, it's spring. The Sukkot festival follows the solemnity of Yom Kippur, and commemorates the forty years that Israelites wandered the desert before they reached the Promised Land. Sukkah (hut) was the name given to the makeshift shelter they lived in. Traditionally in Jewish households the family eats in the Sukkah for the seven days of Sukkot.

But there was no space for a Sukkah in Rabbi Msitshana's garden so he had brought the garden into his home. This was Sukkot Soweto style. The rabbi told the story of the Israelites fleeing Egypt with such passion and conviction; it was as if it was the story of his own life. And indeed, his personal tale had all the makings of an epic testament to a full life.

As a bright and curious boy of seven, Vuyisile, born in 1927, had worried his Methodist parents with inexplicable dreams of Roman numerals in the sky. Distraught, they dragged him off to the 'mfundisi', the minister, then to sangomas and tribal elders. None could figure him out and none could answer his puzzling questions about the Old Testament.

When the world was at war, Vuyisile's friends all wanted to join and fight the demon Hitler. Reluctantly he went along too. The Afrikaner recruitment officer was distinctly unimpressed with this spindly 16-year-old trying to pass himself off as eighteen years old. '*Vat daardie kaffertjie. Hy sal vrek in*

Noord Afrika,' (Take that young 'kaffir' he'll rot in North Africa), the rabbi recalls him saying, with a chuckle. 'I ended up fighting in El Alamein where we were ambushed by the Germans who captured us and sent us off to a prisoner of war camp in Poland,' he told me.

And so the young Xhosa man found his faith in the wartime rubble of Poland. It was only in the throes of the Second World War that he began to see the light. He spoke of his dreams to some Hasidic Jews he had befriended in the Polish prisoner of war camp and, though the concept of proselytising was anathema to them, strange things happen in war. The young Sowetan began an intensive conversion while under the control of the Nazis. 'I used to have these visions. I would see the sky opening up and the word Deuteronomy would appear with a big seven and a small five,' recounted the rabbi. 'It was explained to me by these Jewish people that it was a command from God and it was written in chapter seven verse five of Deuteronomy.'

From 1943 to the war's end, and until they were released by the Russians in 1946, he studied the Torah and Hebrew fervently. He even got engaged to a Jewish girl. He vowed he would return to her. But once back in South Africa where apartheid was starting to take hold it became impossible for him to leave. The girl died in a plane crash on her way to Israel in 1949, the rabbi was refused a passport and permission to attend her funeral. But throughout the upheaval of the apartheid years, it was a dream he never let go: going to Israel and marrying a Jewish girl. He was married unhappily and briefly to a Methodist woman, and he built up a strong Jewish congregation of thousands in Soweto.

But all good tales need a twist. After 1976 he was detained for his part in giving refuge to young activists, and then sent to Robben Island for five years. By the time he returned to Soweto, all had changed. Lost and leaderless in their urban wilderness, most of his followers abandoned the faith, leaving only a couple of hundred loyal to Judaism. Yet Rabbi Msitshana brought up his three children as strict Jews, and kept a kosher kitchen, closely advised and aided by Hasidic Rabbis from Williamsburg in the United States. He translated the Torah into five African languages and struggled to win over the white rabbis of Johannesburg.

With all this determination he still had a niggling feeling of emptiness that bothered him. He yearned to travel to Israel and find that nice Jewish girl, even though he was well over fifty years old. It made sense: the chances of him living with a white, Jewish girl in South Africa of the day, seemed beyond absurd. He was undeterred. 'You just cannot live without a kosher wife,' he told me at the time.

My article was published in the *Sunday Express* (a paper that was forced to close, with the *Rand Daily Mail*, two years later in 1985). I waited for any reaction, but did not expect the endearing response of the Johannesburg Jewish community. While they found it altogether impossible to accept him as a real rabbi (despite his story and certificates), a group of Jewish people approached the Israeli airline company El Al and persuaded it to sponsor his trip to Israel to find a wife.

Here I should tell you that he found a kosher wife, and lived happily ever after. Yet, sadly, he failed. But his story lives on as a testimony to a township of surprises, with secrets tucked away in matchbox homes.

Sarah Crowe has worked as a foreign correspondent, a television executive and presenter, based in Johannesburg, London and Stockholm. She now works as a media consultant for UN agencies and the World Bank. She met Soweto's rabbi early in her career.

Betty's Joint

Nicol Degli Innocenti

It's only ten o'clock in the morning on an unusually wet weekday in Diepkloof, one of Soweto's decidedly ungentrified areas, but Betty Moloi already has customers. Four men chatting around a plastic table in what used to be her garage ask for beer and a smoke. They buy cigarettes one at a time, paying in coins; they buy beer on credit. Betty does not mind: she knows the morning clients are all unemployed. 'They always pay me back because they want to keep coming here,' she says with a grin. 'My place has got quite a reputation in the neighbourhood.'

Betty opened her shebeen in 1962, soon after she moved to the little one-storey brick house at 4049B, Zone 3, Diepkloof. She began selling beer to neighbours and acquaintances from her tiny sitting room and kitchen, but quickly moved 'Betty's Joint' to the garage, turning the tin-roofed structure into a bar to accommodate more people. Business was good from the start, she says, especially at weekends: 'I always open at eight in the morning and close at ten in the evening, but on Friday and Saturday night it is always so crowded I let them stay until midnight.'

This is one of thousands of shebeens in Soweto. Nono Mutasi, area sales manager for South African Breweries, lives and works in the township and knows it like the back of his hand. 'There are a thousand shebeens I know about,' he says, 'but my guess is there are another four thousand out there. For every one that closes two spring up.'

Betty's Joint, which Nono visits regularly, is different from most. She runs a traditional, conservative place. There are no spirit coolers or other trendy drinks in the two big glass-fronted fridges: the choice is between different brands of South African beer. Customers who want a bit of a kick prefer the stronger Carling Black Label, others stick to Hansa or Castle lagers. Unlike many new shebeens in Soweto, where girls and boys drink together, Betty's Joint is strictly a men-only establishment. 'I don't want women here. Women cause trouble,' she says emphatically. 'I caused trouble too when I was young. Lots of trouble,' she adds with a girlish giggle. She clearly enjoys being the only woman in the crowd, and though she is past seventy her eyes still have a mischievous twinkle.

When she was young her clients came to her for the beer and for her dancing. 'I used to do lots of jiving and singing and clowning around. They were happier times then, maybe because I used to like a drink myself,' she laughs. Now her customers come for the beer and for her company. 'Even when I would like to sit quietly in my kitchen and leave them to it they call me out. They want me to tell them stories of what life was like years ago. I make them laugh.'

Betty is worried about when she will have to retire. 'I don't like saying exactly what my age is but I can tell you I was born in 1930,' she says. Her granddaughter will take over

76

and Betty's Joint will lose its character. Her most faithful customers are worried too. 'They keep telling me I must stay. We don't want young men coming here to see your grandchild and changing the place, they say. They are right, you know. Youngsters get drunk and have fights, they are rude, throw cigarette butts on the floor and they refuse to leave when it's time.'

She has made some concessions to modernity, though: the high-tech jukebox on the wall now plays the latest kwaito hits as well as classic jazz and the African songs she used to jive to. She might succumb soon and buy a large-screen television, she says: 'Simply because when there is a big soccer match even my most faithful customers don't come here.'

Her favourite clients are the married ones. 'Even if they are drunk and having fun, when it gets late I tell them they must go home to their wives and they scuttle,' she says. 'The ones who don't have anyone waiting for them want to sit here and drink until dawn.' Her customers are all Sotho or Zulu-speakers from the neighbourhood. Occasionally a stranger walks past, notices the place and walks in. 'I welcome all Africans, as long as they behave, but in forty-two years I have never had a white person come here to drink.'

Under apartheid she did see whites – the policemen. 'The same guys from the liquor squad used to come every week and take me away because I did not have a licence. Every week I would be arrested and told off. I always said sorry, I was wrong, then I came back and opened the shebeen again.' But there was no harassment and no unpleasantness, she insists: 'I never had to spend the night in prison. They were very understanding: they came every Friday to raid the place but they were willing to wait until the Tuesday for me to pay the fine, because they knew I had the money after the weekend's takings. It really wasn't so rough.'

The biggest change she experienced after the end of apartheid was the sudden disappearance of the liquor squads.

Out of habit, however, she still buys only a few cases of beer at a time. 'Just in case they come back and take it away, like they used to do. The white policemen always took away my beer because I did not have a licence,' she says. 'I have often wondered where they took it, but my guess is they drank it pretty quickly!'

The picture she paints of her neighbourhood is one some would struggle to link to Soweto's image. 'It is quiet and friendly, mostly families just struggling to find work and feed their children. I have never been robbed and have never experienced crime.' In the four decades that she has been running her shebeen both South Africa and Soweto have changed a lot but her neighbourhood, she says, is almost the same.

Just a little poorer: 'I don't have anything bad to say about the government. It is my government. All I can say is there were more jobs under apartheid. People had more money, they did not have to buy beer on credit all the time. But I really would not want to go back.'

Nicol Degli Innocenti has been South Africa correspondent for the *Financial Times* since 1999, based in Johannesburg. Before that she worked for *Il Sole* 24 *Ore*, Italy's financial daily, first on the foreign desk and then as Asia editor. As she has two young children, in the evenings she is now more likely to be found clutching a bottle of milk at home than a bottle of beer in a shebeen.

78

The celebrations have fallen quiet

Anne Dissez

It is June 16, 1994, in the wake of the ANC electoral victory that marks the death of apartheid. Sowetans emerge from a string of celebrations that rock the township. A dozen women in mourning clothes, shawls over their heads, walk slowly around the humble grave of Hector Petersen, one of the first to die during historic student protests just under twenty years before. As usual they mutter, and at times sing struggle songs. But this particular morning is different. The anniversary was always celebrated in the midst of violence, right up to 1990, when the apartheid regime legalised all opposition parties, including the most important African National Congress, and freed all political prisoners. Now there is more freedom, but the sadness of these women is more striking than ever.

For the first time since he was released from jail, the most famous political prisoner of all is not here with his supportive presence. For over a month, Nelson Mandela has been the

State President of all South Africans, and he is already building his policy of reconciliation. Soweto is no longer his main political ground, and the activities of ANC leaders have shifted to Pretoria and the President's Union Buildings. But the absence of their brother and leader leaves a bitter taste in the mouths of the mothers of the children of the Soweto uprising.

A few weeks before there was no bitterness at St Philip Church, in Soweto's Moletsane area. There Father Lafont is celebrating his last mass under apartheid. The church is packed; the mood is exultant. Overflowing joy is carried by a youth choir that sustains a quick pace. There is no difference now between religious hymns and struggle songs: the parishioners dance as they pray; the widows in charge of parish social work catch their feet in long purple robes. They swing along as black power fists rise all over the church. Now, this *is* bliss!

The choir starts singing, *Senzeni-na – what have we done*, a traditional song that blacks in the townships sang when, in September 1977, they heard about the death of Steve Biko, leader of the Black Consciousness Movement. He was killed during torture in police custody, where he had been kept since his arrest following the Soweto uprising. '*Senzeni-na*' is a song in which the singers say their only crime is being black. As they sing, just three days before elections, they expect to get back their land. The passion in their voices, the power of the song and flows of emotional tears, all bear witness to the magnitude of the coming victory.

But tears are quickly wiped away as the new South African flag is brought in. This flag was made by a group of artists. The priest unfurls, raises, and swings it high above the parishioners' heads. As it happens, the flag had been adopted by a government still made up of whites only, just a few days before elections. It was supposed to show that, whatever the result, the days of racism and of this 'world apart' were definitely over.

But it was impossible to find the official version of the flag. Only a few had been put together by the government services. Was it lack of time, lack of means, or tardiness of reluctant civil servants who feared the changes to come? On that particular day the flags that stroked parishioners' heads had been sewn together in an art centre called Amakhono, meaning 'talent' in Zulu and Xhosa. The artists worked in a property on the edge of Soweto, once the residence of a mine manager and one of the oldest houses in the region. It was put at the disposal of black artists by a mine owner in 1992 and it foretold the spirit of reconciliation that is so dear to Nelson Mandela.

But all celebrations come to an end, even those in Soweto. Today the township has shed its ghetto rags: over the years roads have been tarred, there is running water in all the houses, the streets are lit up. So too are all the matchbox houses built during the apartheid days. Supermarkets have sprouted within the confines of Soweto. As for political leaders, they have moved from the township and settled in former whites-only areas. At times they go back to visit relatives and parents who remain faithful to their history.

Yet if Soweto looks increasingly like a pretty suburban area, it is still touched by poverty. Misery is rampant, and not only in the squatter camps. The backyards of matchbox houses are crammed with people in makeshift sheds of tin and wooden planks. Unemployment and AIDS trigger brooding fears, and threaten to destroy families. And whereas the struggle against apartheid once brought Sowetans together, today, like many other people, they are on their own, trying to cope with dire and overwhelming circumstances.

In churches priests still call on people to love one another. But in these early days of the third millennium, hope, a boundless feeling that used to carry people through, is draining away. In its place are pain and sorrow. The pain of surviving without a job; the sorrow of children orphaned by AIDS who become heads of their families long before reaching adulthood.

The huge and sprawling black city is no longer the South African capital that it used to be. It was once the capital, too, for anti-apartheid militants worldwide. Soweto, for sure, has lost some of its aura. The struggle is over and reconciliation is accepted, though with some difficulty. Struggle songs and religious hymns no longer blend together in the churches. The good ladies of the parishes in their purple robes still have a long way to go to relieve their fellow humans of all their misery.

As a journalist, Anne Dissez worked for *Radio France International* first in Algeria, then, after 1993, in South Africa. She writes for the French catholic daily *La Croix*. She is presently the Southern Africa correspondent for *Africa #1*, the French speaking radio based in Libreville, Gabon.

Christmas Eve

John Dludlu

It was Christmas Eve of 2003. Without knowing it, I had finally succumbed. A group of colleagues and old college friends had just finished burying Mr Mafata, the father of Mongadi, a friend and colleague at the *Sowetan*. We had had the lunch at the family's house – part of the burial ritual. As mourners began making their journeys back home, we regrouped for an 'after tears' just around the corner from the Mafatas' home. The place was Nambitha's, a tavern on Vilakazi Street.

Mongadi, the paper's social affairs news editor, had tried for months to get me to hold one of the many business meetings that come with the job at Masakeng, another famous watering hole in Mofolo, opposite the famous Eyethu Cinema in Soweto. For me, the cinema is emblematic of Soweto of the eighties. But, somehow, town or suburban restaurants, particularly those around Rosebank, Melville and Sandton, always seemed more convenient than the fifteen minutes it would take to get to Masakeng or Wandie's.

Rosebank is trendy. That's where you want to be seen. And you are likely to bump into the right crowd. Take the Park Hyatt, the upmarket hotel. That's where major empowerment transaction deals are struck. Or The Grace, if you want to be discreet with your investment banker eyeing your next babe. Same story with Sandton's Gazebo, a fashionable coffee shop now revamped into Upper West Side. But if you are still keen on exclusivity, you should try Melrose Arch. All these places have benefited from the decline of downtown Johannesburg which, ironically, coincided with the collapse of apartheid. They are part of the new South Africa and appear to derive their significance from the personalities who grace them. They are part of the new history. This status must be threatened by the push by the provincial government of Gauteng to revive the City of Johannesburg.

Back to Nambitha's. It is firmly rooted in Soweto. Though a new phenomenon, it is safely ensconced in history. A stone's throw away you can stroll to the Hector Petersen Memorial – erected in honour of Hector Petersen, the youth thought to be the first victim of the June 16, 1976 uprising – and embrace the revolutionary spirit. Not too far down, you get a second opportunity to shore up your anti-apartheid credentials by paying homage to the suffering of another struggle veteran, the one and only Mrs Winnie Madikizela-Mandela, ex-wife of Nelson Mandela, South Africa's first post-apartheid and black African president. She has defied the exodus of the black elite to suburbia.

Unlike in the other African eateries in suburbia, Nambitha's waiting staff, like that of other such Soweto taverns, is black African South African. This means native South African blacks. This has its own little upsides. Chief among these must be the fact that if you don't like your maize meal porridge, you can argue for hours about why it is too soft. Or you can haggle how you want your chicken. But you need not worry about offending the staff. If these differences prove too wide and deep, then you can just switch onto one of the vernaculars to settle them. Zimbabwe's Ndebeles fleeing their repressive government steer clear of Soweto's pubs; so too Bulgarians.

But as an indigenous black African South African you can help staff with a bit of marketing and making the European and Asian guests feel even more welcome. Nambitha is one of the symbols of modern-day Soweto. The narrow street provides ample open-air parking for the tourist buses and minibuses. 'Chief, you can park anywhere. It's safe,' says one of the staff as you try to park your luxury German sedan in front of one of the neighbour's gates, where you can see it.

This message of safety and security, also a new characteristic of today's Soweto, is repeated in various parts where there are such taverns. 'People park their cars as far as that field without any trouble,' says a waitress at KwaThabeng (on the hill), another tavern in Pimville's upmarket section of Bester (pronounced Bestah).

Apart from curious foreigners, more black South Africans are frequent patrons of these places. They go not necessarily for business meetings. But they go there to unwind and watch Bafana Bafana, the national football team, disappoint them one more time. At the time of writing, the team had just been kicked out of the Africa Cup of Nations. If it is not soccer that is discussed then the gyrations of the nation's currency, the Rand, and its effects on ordinary people is debated there with passion.

Our inaugural meeting at Nambitha began as an impromptu 'after tears', unusual because these normally take place at a relative's house. But, it soon evolved into an assessment of the real state-of-the-nation: a thorough discussion on the future of the black elite, politics, the professional class and, of course, black economic empowerment. And a very South African group was formed that night by these friends, an advertising executive, a banker, entrepreneur, marketing executive and a

85

newspaper editor. We agreed to form a *stokvel* (a savings-investment scheme) and named it after this joint, promising that all meetings will be held there.

Taverns represent hope about Soweto, once threatened by the spurt of shopping malls. A revival of Soweto that is taking place without a legislative nudge. Triggered by the rich sense of history. In time, with more middle-class black Africans succumbing to what Mongadi might call a new economic patriotism, the accidental 'after tears' will be replaced by tearful celebrations of the township. But only if the new black elite is not too busy or distracted to drive this rejuvenation.

John Dludlu, a graduate of Rhodes University in Grahamstown, is Editor of the *Sowetan*. Prior to joining the *Sowetan*, he worked for nearly ten years at *Business Day* in various capacities: trade writer, Associate Editor, Africa Editor, Managing Editor and acting Deputy Editor.

The Pelican Club

Richard Dowden

The Pelican Club was run by a big cheerful Mozambican called Lucky. I doubt I could find my way to it now, even if it still exists. I went at night anyway. Those were the days when whites needed permission to go to Soweto. I had met some people in the music business in Johannesburg. That was 1979. Most of the bands they recorded were white; pale, plonky mimics of British and American rock bands. But they also were trying to break into the black music scene in Soweto.

I loved the music of other parts of Africa I had visited. Bar jukeboxes everywhere blared out subtle Congolese rhythms and silvery tunes and at formal Saturday night dances in every small town there would be live music from travelling bands. To me, white South Africans were so lucky to be in Africa but they had inexplicably cut themselves off from the best bits of the continent. My experience of Africa was warm, friendly and funny. If its thrilling music didn't force you to dance, its giggly girls would come and drag you to your feet. Oh, said my friends in the music business, you need to go to the Pelican Club then.

The next day I made my way down to the West Rand Administration Board at the bottom end of Johannesburg to obtain a permit. On the second floor in a sparse office I found a Mr Phillips reading a newspaper spread out across an empty desk. He took out a form and asked me why I wanted to go, who I would be visiting, which day and hour I would go, which route I would take, the make, colour and registration number of the car I would be using. The thoroughness of apartheid still astounds. When the huge form was filled, he told me to come back in a week to collect the permit and returned to his newspaper. In contrast to the queues of blacks appearing in the magistrates' courts every day charged with being in a white area illegally, I may have been the only white asking to visit Soweto that day, that week, perhaps even that year.

My first attempt to go was thwarted by an attack on the police station opposite the Pelican the night before. Too dangerous, Lucky said over the phone. So we went the following Saturday; two whites and a mixed-race woman who knew the way. At the time she was disguising herself as white so she could live in the northern suburbs, but she chose to be black that night. We arrived at the club which lay slightly down a slope from the embattled, floodlit police station. Lucky welcomed us warmly and gave us each a tumbler of neat gin. Then he announced our presence over the DJ system which got us a round of applause. Smartly dressed young men and women came over and greeted us. This was three years since the uprising, they told us, and no whites had ventured to the club since. But two years after the death of Steve Biko when Black Consciousness was still the motivating philosophy of resistance to apartheid, these young Sowetans were going out of their way to welcome a couple of whites who crossed the apartheid boundary – if only for an evening's drinking and dancing in their city.

The music however was disappointing; American soul and Western pop. No one had heard of Congolese except Lucky and he said he didn't have any. If South Africa's whites were cut off from Africa, so too were blacks.

A group of girls came over and asked me to dance. Two boys joined us and formally asked my permission to dance with the two girls I had come with. I bought some beers and the bottles were passed from mouth to hand round the dance floor. Lucky interrupted the music to announce that someone had lost a watch. 'Whoever finds that watch, brothers and sisters, has got to give it back.' A couple of minutes later he announced it had been found and returned. 'Thank you, brothers and sisters,' he said, 'and a thank you to those who caused that disturbance last week.' There was a roar of *amandla* and a show of clenched fists across the dance floor. It was one of the few black political manifestations I saw on that visit.

Lucky had an extra reason for hating the police. The Pelican Club did not have an alcohol licence and the police had raided recently and fined him five hundred rand. That was three nights' takings. Later in the evening he brought us plates of meat and pap which we ate with our fingers. When my friend asked for a napkin Lucky told her to find the man with the nicest looking shirt on the dance floor, 'Go and dance with him and hold him real close.'

A few years later I went to Soweto to visit the person who to me was the real Mother of the Nation, Albertina Sisulu, wife of the African National Congress leader, Walter Sisulu. I met her in the shack that served as the reception for the surgery for Dr Aswat, who was later murdered. Bleak is the word that sums up Soweto to me and that little hut seemed to be in the bleakest part, surrounded by rubbish and wretchedness. Inside, dressed in a nurse's uniform if I remember correctly, was one of the warmest, brightest human beings I have ever met. In a slow, motherly sort of way she made me a cup of tea and chatted about the state of things, the people she served and the city. Between the lines she was, incidentally, giving me a clear analysis of the state of the resistance. At one point she went through her own family on her fingers starting with her thumb, Walter, then Max, ticking them off – prison, exile, prison, prison, exile then she came to one who was at university. She sniffed and looked up with a twinkling eye: 'I don't know where I went wrong with that one.'

Richard Dowden is a writer and the Director of the Royal African Society in London. He has been involved in Africa for thirty years as a teacher and a journalist and has travelled extensively on the continent. He has worked for the *Times*, the *Independent* and the *Economist*, among others.

Queer Soweto

Mark Gevisser

'When you're gay, you're beautiful, right?' asks Pastor Tsietsi Thandekiso at the height of his sermon. When his congregation, one hundred or so young black men and women, does not answer, he volleys back, 'Has somebody got a problem here?', his voice slightly inflected, Southern-Baptist camp. 'Because if you got a problem we'll lay our hands on you and solve the problem. But you'll still be gay. No one in this church is a mistake. If you got a problem it's in your head; it's not because you are gay.'

Tsietsi Thandekiso, who died in early 1998 of AIDS-related illness, founded his Hope And Unity Metropolitan Community Church (HUMCC) in April 1994, literally days after the first democratic elections. Ten years later, it remains the most enduring institution in urban South African black gay life; the reason for its popularity precisely its use of the style and the liturgy of the African Independent churches, fusing charismatic

Christianity with local African prayer styles and singing.

The HUMCC now meets at the Anglican Church in Mayfair; for years, its home was the ballroom of the seventh floor of the Harrison Reef Hotel in Hillbrow, above The Skyline – Johannesburg's oldest gay bar. The Skyline has changed colour along with the neighbourhood; although it has declined in recent years, in the years that the HUMCC ran its mission out of the Harrison Reef, it was the epicentre of Johannesburg's black gay scene: black drag queens, rent boys, professionals and township kids gathered there in droves on Friday and Saturday nights. With a jukebox and tacky modular seventies decor, it was one of those environments that was perfectly retro without having the slightest intention of being so.

But if the Harrison Reef rebounded with the gay anthems of the seventies on Saturday nights, it gave way to a very different aural interference on Sunday afternoons: the gospel-chanting, chair-slapping, Satan-slaying, yea-saying evangelism of the church; lurid faith superimposed upon a shabby hotel room converted into a place of worship with a wooden cross wrapped in tinfoil, a keyboard, some pink tablecloths and a bouquet of flowers.

The prayer, this wintry May Sunday in 1997, is particularly fervent, because today's service is the anniversary of the marriage of two young Soweto women, Pretty Robiana and Sbongile Malaza. The couple shuffles into the room to the rhythm of an African hymn, Pretty in a military-style navy suit with gold braiding and epaulettes, Sbongile in a girlish pink appliquéd dress. There is no doubt as to the gender roles in their marriage: Pretty is burly and as aggressive as any African man is meant to be; Sbongile, still in the throes of adolescent acne, is almost a caricature of the traditional African wife: she does not look you in the eye, she answers in whispers. They call each other 'husband' and 'wife'.

They grew up on the same street in Emdeni, one of Soweto's rougher neighbourhoods. Sbongile is nineteen years old, and is in her final year of high school; she has been raised by her grandparents, a domestic worker and a retired security guard. Pretty is twenty-four and unemployed, the daughter of a single parent, a nursing sister; she is of the 'Glow Generation', the first generation of black kids to have come out in the townships in the wake of 'Gays and Lesbians of Witwatersrand', the organisation founded by the charismatic Simon Nkoli. Ostracised from her family's church because she refused to wear the women's uniform and came instead in jacket and tie, Pretty found out about the HUMCC through a magazine article. She joined the church, and decided that she wished to marry her sweetheart.

Gay South Africans have constitutional equality, and a series of court rulings have meant that same-sex couples can be married in all but name. Nonetheless, Thandekiso agreed to marry Pretty and Sbongile before God. The two were already ostracised from their families; Sbongile's grandmother, who had worked for a white lesbian couple, told the girl that it was 'Satanic' and 'un-African'. When Sbongile's grandfather turned a gun on Pretty and assaulted both of them, the young couple fled the township, spending some time in a battered women's shelter. Later, meeting her on the street, the old man fired three shots at his granddaughter's 'husband', narrowly missing her head.

Laying charges of attempted murder with the police, Pretty met an unexpected response. The station commander, a woman, told her, 'the constitution is here now. You people have decided you want to lead this life and it comforts you, so let us call the family together and discuss it and make peace.' She convened a meeting with both families and the chairman of the local street committee who said, according to Pretty, 'this is a surprise to me. I have never seen this before, but there is nothing I can do about it'. After the meeting the station commander gave Pretty a document to sign to say that she was responsible for Sbongile, and told Sbongile's

93

family that there was nothing illegal about the women's union.

Once the marriage had the official stamp of the station commander, the Malaza family changed its tune: they want Pretty to pay them *lobola*, the bride-price that is at the root of African marital union. Nonetheless, the only member from either family to attend the anniversary service was one of Sbongile's sisters: 'We accept our sister,' she said in a brief and shy speech to the church, 'despite what she is.' The night before, Pretty and Sbongile held a party at the Harrison Reef, to which hundreds came: not only fellow-congregants, but neighbours from Soweto – where the couple rents a room in a yard – and even one of Sbongile's teachers, who made a speech and gave a gift.

※

When I visited the HUMCC in 1996, at the height of Robert Mugabe's homophobia, I met two young Zimbabweans in the church. One, Remington Ncube, was a migrant miner working in the Johannesburg area. A deeply religious man, he had been an altar-server in his Catholic church; when his family discovered he was homosexual, he was chased out of home and church. 'I had to leave Bulawayo,' he said, 'and there was only one place to go. It is known all over the continent that Johannesburg is the freest place for black gays . . .'

Thoko Ndlovu comes from Bulawayo too. 'Why am I in Johannesburg?' she asked. 'Well, I picked up one of those pop black magazines in Bulawayo one day, and there was an article about all this terrible sinful activity in Jo'burg. And I said, "Get me on the next bus! I'm going there!" '

Zimbabwe and South Africa are separated by nothing more than the Limpopo river. Zimbabweans and South Africans are the same people, with similar histories and interconnected economies. How is it that their cultures have adopted so

94

different an approach to the same issue? There are many possible explanations: the porous and hybrid nature of urban South African life, where essentialist patriarchy no longer holds much truck; the role of popular culture in South Africa, where gay issues and subjects have become immensely popular on the TV talk show; the influence, particularly, of American ideas and styles in the country.

A lot has to do, too, with the moral authority that the ANC carries. Shortly after the 1994 elections, Glow organiser Polly Motene, who lives in Soweto, told me that 'attitudes have changed among those who read the newspapers, because there has been more publicity about gay people.' Motene's father, for example, was a local ANC activist, 'and he was astonished when he heard about how the ANC supports gay people.' But Motene also offered a caution: 'Most Sowetans haven't heard a thing about the gay clause in the constitution. For them, homosexuality remains a white thing, and we black gays are just freaks, *stabane* with two organs.'

Also shortly after those first elections, Beverly Ditsie, perhaps the first black lesbian Sowetan to come out publicly, explained the downside of ANC support for gay causes: 'Right now there is quite a lot of dissatisfaction on the ground with the government, because it is perceived to be going out of its way to reconcile with whites rather than looking after its own people. And so if you tell people that Mandela supports gay rights, they'll either get angry with you and tell you that you are lying, or they'll just say, "Oh there he goes, looking after everyone except for us again," because of course gayness for them is a white thing, so it's further proof that he is ignoring his own constituency in favour of whites.'

But while she offered a bleak picture of the persistent homophobia in township society, Ditsie did acknowledge that things had changed since 1990 when, as one of the spokespeople of South Africa's first Lesbian and Gay Pride March, she found herself the victim of violent and sustained gay-bashing in her native Soweto after appearing on television. In the late nineties she participated in a proto-Reality TV experiment called 'Livewire', in which six young people from wildly differing backgrounds were thrown together in a commune and videotaped for a few months in a rather spurious sort of guinea pig trial for integration in South Africa. The show attracted much attention, not least because Ditsie – the only black woman in the commune – made no bones about her sexuality.

'I found,' she said, 'that attitudes began to change towards me in Soweto. People began to see me as their representative on the show, because I was black, because I was strong, because I knew what I wanted.' She went onto a radio call-in show to talk about the experience, 'and people would phone in and say, "you really spoke well for us". I'd ask, "who is 'us'?" The answer would sometimes be black people, sometimes women, sometimes gay people. It all becomes one thing, one struggle . . .'

✳

It is 2003, and I am working with two Soweto lesbians to develop a 'Queer Tour' of Johannesburg for the Gay and Lesbian Archives at the University of the Witwatersrand (GALA). Busi Kheswa is an elder of the HUMCC and a researcher at GALA; Nkunzi Nkabinde is a practising *sangoma* (a traditional healer). They are both in their mid-twenties.

We have a dilemma. When foreign gay tourists come to Soweto, they want to see the 'scene': bars, clubs, the 'shebeens' they've heard so much about. And there are none. How can this be possible, given the fact that South Africa is the constitutional leader in gay equality, and the black gay movement is so renowned? We scratch around desperately for a shebeen we might visit, and eventually find one in Orlando East. It is 'straight', but gay people sometimes gather there. There is also a gay professional who lives in Diepkloof Extension, the fanciest part of Soweto, who turns his large home, every now and then, into a dinner-dance club, particularly on June 16, the anniversary of the Soweto uprisings. And, spontaneously, by the word of mouth telegraph, gay street bashes will erupt now and then.

None of these, however, constitutes a 'gay scene' to be shown to visiting pink-pounders. And that, perhaps, is the point about gay and lesbian life in Soweto, as in all urban South African townships: it is integrated into city life rather than coralled off into a western-style gay ghetto, a Chelsea or a Castro Street or a Marais. 'Homophobia in the townships is superficial,' said Tsietsi Thandekiso to me before his death. 'We are living through a time where it's actually not such a big deal to be gay. Go to the township, and you will see in almost every school a group of children who are gay. There are gays on the streets, gays in the taverns. It's become a part of life.'

As we plan the Queer Tour's stops in Soweto, Busi Kheswa tells me that she does not quite agree. It is not so much the homophobia on the streets, although that is a huge problem, particularly for lesbians; rather, it is just the difficulty of being open in your home community. In Soweto, for example, both economic and cultural imperatives mean that you remain in your family home, at least until your marriage, and often afterwards. It's really just about space, and the privacy that middle-class people expect, gay or straight. So young professionals like Busi move to town as soon as they can afford to, and become part of the 'gay scene' there. Soweto is a place you come to on Sundays, to visit your family.

But then there is her friend, Nkunzi. The *sangoma* remains in Soweto because that is where her practice is. We decide that rather than showing visitors 'the gay life' of Soweto, we will simply show them *her* life. And so the bus stops outside her tiny place; a 'family quarters' house converted out of the

97

single-sex barracks of Meadowlands Hostel. The neighbours nod a greeting to the visitors, and we move through the house to a small room off the yard. These are Nkunzi's consulting chambers; the shelves of the tiny room filled with the tools of her trade: the bottles of crushed herbs, the bones, the ceremonial cloths. We sit in a circle, and she tells us about her work. 'They know I am a lesbian, but they do not seem to have much of a problem with it,' she says of her community and her patients. Being a sangoma, too, gives her the protection that other single women living alone might not have: she has powers; she is married to her ancestor, so she is not expected to take a husband.

As we drive around Soweto, Busi and Nkunzi reveal, to the tourists on the bus, the gay thread in Soweto's tapestry. They talk about gay catering companies and *stokvels* (saving societies) and a huge public wedding that took place in Orlando West; about how HIV has ravaged the gay community in particular; about how pioneers such as Simon Nkoli and Bev Ditsie organised young black people into a movement. We drive past Nancefield Hostel and hear about *umkhehlo,* the 'mine-marriages' that used to take place here between migrant labourers far away from their families. We drive past Archbishop Desmond Tutu's home, and hear about the role that he has played in supporting gay equality; we drive past Winnie Mandela's home, and hear how black gay Sowetans protested against her court defence that 'Homosex is not in Black Culture'. We drive along the route that the June 16 marchers took, and hear that one of their leaders became a founder of the HUMCC church, and about how the uprising of 1976 made space for the first generation of openly gay and lesbian men and women.

As we pass through Pimville, I look out of the window and see, outside a shop, a couple of *skesanas* – as effeminate gay men are known – dressed in that creative demi-drag born of scant resources and much imagination: palazzo pants over a pair of low-heeled pumps; a dash of rouge; a sleeveless lycra halter neck. They are engaged in a particularly elaborate snap routine, with expansive hand gestures and wild facial mugs; something between *Sarafina* and Naomi Campbell. I can hear the screeches through the window. The street is crowded. No one is paying them any attention at all.

Mark Gevisser is a Johannesburg-based author and heritage consultant. He is currently involved in the development of Constitution Hill. His biography of Thabo Mbeki is expected to be published in late 2004.

An adventure in technicolour

Anne Hammerstad

Late one winter's day we drove to Soweto. The occasion was Walter Sisulu's funeral, and we wanted to do our bit to make the occasion worthy of the non-racial society the ANC hero sought. The funeral at the Orlando Stadium had all the ingredients of contrast and contradiction we had learnt to expect from living in South Africa for a couple of years. Flashy cars with the beautiful people of the new political elite driving through dusty brown streets of the township. Zimbabwe's Robert Mugabe as a guest of honour at the funeral of a liberation hero who never wanted political power for himself. And a few ornamental white (or pink, really) dots from the northern suburbs scattered across stands otherwise occupied by a solid wall of black Sowetans. Looking around me I had never before in my life felt so different, so outside: so very, very white.

So what, you may ask. What else would you expect from

such a racially divided country? Well, where I grew up I learnt that race is a dirty word. It is okay to identify yourself with being Norwegian, Scandinavian, European (although in South Africa even 'European' has a racial slant), but never as a member of the 'white' race. Then, coming to South Africa, I was told that I can forget understanding the place unless I accept the all-importance of race. A Jo'burg friend one night tried to convince me that the word 'coloured' was not off-limits in a civilised vocabulary. She helpfully provided an example she thought would be familiar. Speaking about the 'coloureds' in South Africa is no different from discussing the 'Norwegian race', she said. Well that's exactly the problem, I thought. What on earth would the 'Norwegian race' be? Some sort of tall blonde creature with a genetic proclivity for multi-lateralism and filter coffee? If you ever come across a Nor-wegian talking about his race, you can be sure he is a neo-Nazi.

Sure, people in different parts of the world use different words to explain similar things. Americans are not as averse to the R-word as are Europeans. Having invented and then lived with the horrible consequences of eugenics, fascism and Nazism, Europe has thoroughly discredited 'race' as a scientific or social means to categorise people. Instead we struggle to come up with ever new terms for the we-group such as 'culture', 'ethnic group', 'ethnies', 'nations', 'people' or 'com-munity' – the latter is the most favoured among European political and social commentators. As one word becomes too loaded with smutty baggage we migrate to another in a perpetual race (no pun intended) to find ways of talking about 'us' and 'them' without appealing to base human habits of xenophobia and intolerance.

Having invented and lived through the depraved system of apartheid, why then do South Africans still cling to the R-word? Is it just that they beat about the bush less than hypocritical and self-satisfied Norwegians? If so, it is in spiteful ignorance of the power of language. Explain everything in terms of race and, voila, race becomes the explanation for everything. Choose the term class instead, and you get a very different picture of South Africa's social and political problems. But the hopeful thing about class is that there is nothing genetic or preordained about which category you fit into.

That's all very fine on paper. But the truth is that Walter Sisulu's funeral did threaten to add one more example to a growing collection of South African experiences that were shaking my non-racial world view.

Walking back to our car after the ceremony, we realised that it had been parked in by two other cars. There was nothing to do but to sit down in the garden of a friendly local man and wait for the owners of the cars to arrive. Luckily, there was more than enough hospitality to go around, so we were quite enjoying our afternoon in Soweto – secretly thinking to ourselves, but not mentioning it out loud, how nicely the telling of this adventure would go down with our friends in the northern suburbs.

There were four of us. Three grown-ups and Adrian, the 14-year-old son of a family that was visiting South Africa for a few weeks. His parents were busy and he wanted to see a real township, so we brought him along. He was a true child of globalisation, a typical example of the new international elite that grows up in several countries, goes to international schools, and as a result feels comfortable and at home in all corners of the world. Bilingual in French and English, with trendy spiky hair, a gentle self-confidence and excellent dribbling skills, he was soon the star of a football match that shaped up between the kids of our host and neighbouring boys and girls.

A couple of hours later, our car free at last, we made our farewells. A serious and shy little girl around ten, who to her delight had been allowed to play football with the bigger

102

boys, went up to Adrian:

'It is a privilege that a white boy like you comes and plays football with us,' she said before she waved him into our waiting car.

A statement like that from a precocious 10-year-old who never lived under apartheid could easily have put the nail in the coffin of my non-racial stubbornness. Perhaps pigment was the easiest way to explain differences after all, at least in South Africa? Was this articulate little girl so impressed by an outsider that she thought it a 'privilege' to be with a boy with white skin?

Yes, except for one thing. Adrian happened to be black. With French, not African, parents, but nevertheless and unmistakably black. I cheerfully re-archived my day in Soweto from black and white to technicolour and began looking forward to the day when that little girl realises that her ideas of black and white are actually a burgeoning class consciousness.

A writer and academic, Anne Hammerstad now works at the South African Institute of International Affairs. She previously wrote for *Dagbladet*, one of Norway's daily newspapers, and has published articles elsewhere. She lives in Johannesburg.

Death in Soweto

Heidi Holland

Traditional Africa comprehends death, the greatest enigma of human experience, more successfully than the West. It does so by bringing the dead back into the world of the living as ancestors. The ritual to sanctify the living dead is conducted after a mourning period and spans several days, usually commencing with a beer and involving the sacrifice of two or more beasts.

'Although black people go to a lot of trouble and expense to bury and mourn their dead, it's a contradiction,' says the Reverend Otto Mbangula, a minister of the Methodist Church in Soweto. 'They don't really believe you die. They believe you go to the bigger family of ancestors. They can call on the ancestors any time, just as the ancestors come to them in dreams all the time.'

Residents of Soweto attend funerals more frequently than any community in the world, especially in a time of AIDS.

Although the township's traumatic history destroyed much of the social fabric that previously held the urban community together, death continues to bring unity to the living. The family, once an unassailable institution, is now frail and often inadequate in day-to-day life; yet it remains powerfully resilient when confronting death. 'It comes down to the fact that they are committed and connected to each other, not in superficial, sentimental ways, but in real solidarity,' says Methodist Bishop Paul Verryn, one of a handful of whites living in Soweto.

'There is no death that cannot be contained by this community. No matter how dreadful the circumstances, the community will be there to carry you through the agony you've got to face. You'll never face it alone. I've very rarely come across a death that is not mourned fully. If you die and nobody comes to mourn you, you must know that the community considers you a very bad person indeed.'

The funeral service for Busisiwe Lilian Matsimbi, born in Soweto in 1944, is held at her home in Phiri. A wizened, bearded priest wearing the blue and white cassock of the Zion Church leads the service in prayer, beneath a striped red tent that is pitched outside the house. Mourners harmonise amen and begin a soft, sad hymn while women huddled around the coffin weep and sway.

Embarking on a passionate sermon, the priest shouts and gesticulates. Nobody stirs. When he is quiet, the congregation begins to sing in English, a haunting hymn often heard in Soweto:

Give your love to Africa, we are brothers all,
Who by sin and slavery long were held in thrall,
Let the white man love the black and when time is passed,
In our Father's home above, all shall meet at last.

Two of Busisiwe's male relatives pay tribute to her. She

worked hard all her life and bore her burdens with courage. She fought for justice and helped people whenever she could. She was calm and truthful; a good wife and mother. When one of the speakers falters, overcome with emotion, the mourners hum, giving him time to recover.

He recalls the day Busisiwe walked to Chris Hani Baragwanath Hospital to visit her dying mother and didn't come home for five days because she couldn't bear to leave the old woman alone. A doctor gave her permission to sleep under the patient's bed until death came.

The other speaker, Busisiwe's son, tells a long story about a job he once had in Johannesburg, which required him to dress up in a Father Christmas suit and distribute leaflets door-to-door. As he walked along suburban streets day after day, whites in cars waved to him. Children ran up to greet him gleefully. When he discussed this puzzling warmth with his mother, she said it was because the suit and the white cotton wool beard covered up his black skin.

A friend of the deceased from a funeral co-operative known as the Peaceful Burial Society – one of thousands of exclusively women's clubs in Soweto in which members pool monthly subscriptions to ensure that they and their families are decently buried – reads the messages on plastic wreaths, holding her candle aloft in a steady hand despite hot wax that spills down her arm.

Leading the funeral procession from the tent, the priest chants exuberantly. As he steps into the sunshine there is a low roll of drums and a troop of slender majorettes in starched yellow and white dresses high-step into the dirt road ahead of the hearse, where they stand to attention.

The chief mourner and her close kin ride in matching grey Cadillac stretch limos as the funeral cortège moves slowly forward, led by the prancing dancers and several young drummers beating time. The rest of the mourners are crammed into three large buses. This is an average funeral by Soweto standards: often six buses are required. Anyone can attend a funeral, whether they knew the deceased or not, a tradition that provides a safety net and at least one square meal a week for the poorest residents.

It is midday. The sun is high and hot. The pace of the drum majorettes quickens until they are running, occasionally springing into the air in a flare of yellow skirts. A siren shrieks from the hearse to warn traffic in the main road ahead.

Avalon Cemetery is a tangle of activity and neglect. Its roads are shallow ditches. Dozens of buses, hearses and mourners' limousines weave their way across the veld separating one stretch of graves from another. Tall weeds obscure the older graves; wreaths tumble about in the wind and the sickly sweet smell of khakibos fills the air.

The hide of the cow which has been slaughtered to feed guests at the funeral feast is laid over the coffin. Busisiwe is lowered into the earth. A concrete slab goes into the grave, a precaution against theft of the casket containing her snuff, cooking pots and the blankets that she will need in the next life. The priest recites his words. The chief mourner screams and falls to the ground, a dark mud stain spreading on a blanket she holds around her despite the heat. Though helped to her feet she falls again. Mourners file slowly past the grave, each with a handful of soil to spill over the coffin. 'Hamba kahle,' they murmur.

Heidi Holland is a journalist and author of books on the South African liberation struggle, Soweto and Africa's traditional belief system. She co-edited, with Adam Roberts, a collection of journalists' stories on Johannesburg entitled *From Jo'burg to Jozi: Stories about Africa's infamous city* (Penguin Books 2002).

From Gwelo to Soweto

Michael Holman

I do not like Soweto. I know that it is almost *de rigueur* to sing its praises. But I just don't like the place. Never have. I have never written a salute to what may be called its 'indomitable spirit', or hailed its 'indefatigable diversity', or praised its 'boundless courage'. This township or suburb or slum, call it what you will, may well be a symbol of gutsy resistance, a grim symptom of apartheid, or deserve its portrayal as one of the worst legacies of white rule.

Not for me. Perhaps I am just being perverse. My friends have been known to call me bloody-minded. But for me there are other, more persuasive monuments to dark days, such as the soulless dormitory of Onverwacht, in the Free State, where black families lost hope, well out of the spotlight that focused on Soweto. And on the scale of sheer human misery, Soweto lags behind the festering favelas of Luanda.

Nor does it match the horrors of the slums of Lagos. Lagos:

now there's a city to reckon with. Rough, tough, raw and powerful. Walk down Broad Street, once lined with banks which long ago migrated to the safety of Ikoyi or Victoria Island. Wander a block inland, and you are in Jankari market. Follow your nose, and you'll find the butchers' stands, awash in blood and offal. 'Like the Somme on a bad day,' said an irreverent colleague.

But Soweto does not inspire me, or intimidate me, as Lagos does.

When it was in the front line of the struggle against apartheid I visited the place, but with no great enthusiasm. Duty took me there. I've accumulated no special anecdotes from the grim urban sprawl. Unlike nearly every journalist of my acquaintance, I have never been mugged, shot at, or car-jacked there.

Today, I do not care to visit its shebeens, however sophisticated or fashionable they might be. I don't find Soweto's contrasts in lifestyles engaging, or its enthusiasms entertaining. I regard the ghettos of wealthy residents, with their expensive houses, not as a triumph of the entrepreneurial spirit but as conspicuous displays of dreadful architectural taste.

So I have had no reason to commemorate or celebrate Soweto – until, that is, some ten years after the elections that marked the end of apartheid.

It took place during one of those guided tours. I think it is a good thing if tourists find time in an itinerary of beaches and game parks to spend a few hours seeing how many black South Africans live. And it was on such a tour that Soweto became indelibly associated with the day that I cracked.

Friends from London were visiting South Africa, and we were a few minutes into a visit to the museum that commemorates Hector Petersen. He was the 13-year-old who was said to be the first to die when some 30 000 students took to the streets of Soweto, protesting against a government edict that all classes were to be taught in Afrikaans.

At the time of his death in 1976 I was a journalist based

in Salisbury (now Harare, in Zimbabwe), and was soon to move to Lusaka in Zambia. The image of that young boy, carried dead or dying in his friend's arms, must be one of the most powerful to emerge from those grim, ghastly days.

But it was not this image, moving as it is, that triggered my distress, which penetrated my professional carapace of detachment. If I was carrying emotional baggage associated with Soweto, I was not aware of it then. It was not this poignant photo that triggered memories of the past in a way that left me vulnerable.

It was something mundane and banal.

We had entered the museum together, but soon I was separated from the group. I lingered near the start of the display, fascinated as well as repelled, transported to the days of my youth in Rhodesia, as I listened to an interview. It was a filmed interview, on a loop, and so the images and the words recurred at regular intervals.

A white woman, in her mid-thirties, speaking with those clipped southern African vowels, was setting out her concerns about majority rule. I cannot remember any more detail. But in familiar code-word language, in a reasonable tone, quite matter of fact, as if spelling out the obvious, she justified an evil system. Over, and over, and over again.

It became the voice I had heard throughout my youth, and beyond. I watched and listened, mesmerised by this voice from the fifties.

Then it hit me. I was overwhelmed by a great wash of sadness for generations lost during the scourge of apartheid. Not just for the millions who died, directly or indirectly, victims of war or preventable disease; but for the might-have-beens, the should-have-beens, the could-have-beens: the unread writers, the unheard musicians, the uncelebrated athletes, the talented and the ordinary – lost to Africa, lost to the world, sacrificed to prejudice.

Suddenly and unexpectedly, I was weeping. Or to put it

bluntly, I sobbed. There was none of the dignity that can be associated with the word 'weep'. These were not discreet tears, not dignified drops, rolling down my cheeks. My shoulders shook and my nose ran copiously.

So why, I still wonder, was I so uncontrollably moved?

For over thirty years I have been a journalist. I like to think that I am as hardbitten as the next hack. My notebook has recorded racism and its consequences all this time, drawing on my childhood in Gwelo, Rhodesia, the events that followed Ian Smith's unilateral declaration of independence, and the export of South Africa's battle to Angola, South West Africa and Mozambique. It was a grim and ghastly era, the sixties, the seventies, the eighties, until that loop was broken in the early nineties.

But when I visited the Hector Petersen museum in 2003 my guard was down. My notebook had been left behind, literally and metaphorically. And over the years that notebook has served as the great anaesthetic. It has functioned as a mind-numbing filter through which tragedy is kept at a distance. It ensured that compassion takes second place to more pressing concerns: how much space for the story, how to write it, when to file it.

This time there was no deadline to distract me, no byline to seduce me, no dateline to add to my collection. For the first time in many years, I was off duty.

And although the link may be tenuous, that is how I remember Soweto. The Hector Petersen museum. The place where I blubbed. But I write this dry-eyed. My memory has served as my notebook. The protective artifice of my trade still works.

Michael Holman was brought up in Zimbabwe and has written on and from Africa for the *Financial Times* since 1975. He lives in London.

111

Rugby

Dominic Hughes

When I was a teenager growing up in the suburbs of London in the eighties, South Africa seemed to be on the television news every night. And more often than not the reports would come from the townships, the scene of some new atrocity. And it was Soweto that stuck in my mind and became the iconic township. Sitting in the safety of my parents' home, I saw images of boys and girls my age, standing in the dusty streets, throwing rocks at the police. Sometimes they were shot at in return, and then the limp bodies of the victims would be gathered up by crying relatives, or their arms and legs would flail as they were carried to safety. I remember one report that followed a crowd that had found a suspected police informer. They hung a rubber tyre around his neck and set it on fire. The camera cut away, returning only to film the aftermath. It was a powerful, moving piece of television.

Like many people my age I joined the anti-apartheid

movement in Britain. At Bristol University my girlfriend was one of the organisers of the group, dragging me from my bed on a Saturday morning to picket the Shell petrol station on Cotham Road. Shell had kept its business ties in the old South Africa, despite international pressure. For Thatcher's Children the fight against apartheid was *the* defining political struggle of our times. We bought Free Nelson Mandela by the Special AKA, we boycotted South African wine, Cape apples and, yes, Shell petrol stations.

So I was excited to be driving into Soweto for the first time in 2004. The scale surprised me – I had no idea Soweto was so huge. The two massive cooling towers of the power station, covered in colourful murals, dominated the skyline. Dusty roads between the rows and rows of houses had been replaced by neat, paved streets. Parts looked like the suburbia where I grew up. In some areas there were two-storey brick houses with tiled roofs and a BMW or Mercedes parked outside. Our cameraman, Gugulakhe Radebe, said somewhat plaintively that Soweto no longer looked like the place where he grew up. I'm not convinced, though, that he was entirely disappointed.

Some areas were a bit skanky. By the taxi rank a group of men were chopping up what appeared to be sheep's heads. A pile of skulls lay on the ground, all teeth and bones stripped of flesh, reeking in the midday sun. But even here I was reminded more of Georgetown in Barbados than the front line in the fight against apartheid of my imagination.

We were in Soweto to do a piece for the BBC on black rugby players. A decade after the collapse of apartheid black players still struggle to make it into the national team. Maybe that is why the Springboks had just had such a miserable season on the pitch, failing at the Rugby World Cup in Australia. Off the field they hadn't fared much better, battling accusations of racism within the team and the administration. Yet a recent survey claimed that now seventy per cent of rugby players in South Africa are black. Looking into the story, I had casually mentioned that if a rugby club existed in Soweto, it would be an ideal place to see some black rugby players in action. I was amazed when our researcher announced that she had found exactly that. So off we went to see the Soweto Rugby Club.

We bumped along a dusty track behind a football stadium. I had lost my bearings in the maze of streets and low brick housing. This felt like a less salubrious part of town. Then ahead of us a fence, topped with razor wire, and a gate. We drove in.

I was expecting a dozen or so players. Instead there were at least fifty. They were young, very fit and very good. This was preseason training and we watched them run up and down the field as their coach, Donald Ngwenya, barked out instructions and encouragement. The ground itself was a large oval, and the surface was hard, tussocky grass, with the occasional bare patch of red earth. But there were floodlights, and the players went at it with fierce enthusiasm. They moved on to ball-handling practice, hopping over a series of tackle bags before crashing into two players holding protective pads. They were absolutely ferocious, yelling, leg pumping, hitting the two tacklers hard. It was exhilarating and made for great TV and radio. Listening to the sound recording later in the office the hairs stood up on the back of my neck.

We interviewed Donald as the players carried on with their exercises. A handsome man with a fantastic smile, he told me that racism is still rife in South African rugby. His players got it on the pitch all the time and he had been abused by other coaches. 'It takes a long time to change people's mindsets,' he said. And yet the players of Soweto Rugby Club are passionate about a game that to all intents and purposes is trying hard to keep them out. None of the young guys training were being paid, but they were giving it their all. As an English fan, a shiver ran down my spine when I thought how good a South African team could be that harnessed these players.

Later I phoned the girlfriend from Bristol University who has since become my wife. She was as excited as I was to hear that I had actually been to Soweto, that city whose name was so resonant for us both. 'Did you get photos?' she asked. I did, but I doubt they do it justice. Instead I have the memory of fifty rugby players, training under the floodlights to play a game that seems not to want them, but loving it nonetheless.

Dominic Hughes reported on British politics for six years for the BBC, then joined the BBC World Service and served as its Sydney correspondent from 1999 to 2003. Now living in London with his wife Sophie, he made his first trip to South Africa in February 2004.

Dolly's house in Orlando West

Nicole Itano

Dolly Hlophe meets me at her door with a glowing smile, dressed in an eye-piercing, fluorescent green South African tourism T-shirt. Her tidy house is small and ornately decorated with African masks, handmade pillows and heavy curtains. Outside, late flowers of summer fade in her well-tended garden and shouts of children, just home from school, fill the streets.

The cosy prosperity of Dolly's neighborhood, the fabled Orlando West, is a far cry from images of an angry and seething Soweto that once filled television screens around the world. In many ways the neighbourhood seems safer and more normal than my own in Johannesburg's heavily fortified northern suburbs. The only neighbour I know is the one whose car I backed into just after I arrived. But in Orlando West many houses, like Dolly's, have no security walls and there is not an electric fence in sight. Neighbours greet each other warmly and chastise each other's children for misbehaviour.

A decade ago, foreign correspondents based in Johannesburg could navigate Soweto like old hands. South Africa was one of the world's big stories and they daily went to places like Orlando West to see the drama of apartheid played out. Today, many of us venture to Soweto rarely, too rarely probably to truly understand how far this country has come. In part, this is because the gaze of the world has moved on, to other conflicts in other parts of the world. But it also reflects the declining significance to South Africa of Soweto, which is no longer the home of the country's black elite.

Nevertheless, as the tenth anniversary of Nelson Mandela's election approached, I decided to head to Orlando West, once the home of Soweto's intelligentsia and a hotbed of anti-apartheid activism. I wanted to see whether freedom had indeed brought rewards to South Africa's old black elite, who had much to lose but also the most to gain from democracy. I found, as one finds all over South Africa, reasons for both hope and despair.

Dolly Hlophe is typical of Orlando West's old families. She and her husband formed part of South Africa's tiny apartheid-era black middle class, rich by Soweto standards though not by white ones. Given land by the government in the aftermath of the 1976 riots, they built their three-bedroomed home themselves, adding new rooms and small luxuries over the years.

Dolly became an African National Congress activist, one of the many rank and file who kept the movement alive at home while its leaders languished in prison or fought for freedom from exile. One of her daughters was educated in an ANC school in Tanzania.

Today, she has no doubts about the benefits of freedom. Her daughters, both in their twenties, have college degrees and good jobs; opportunities that she never had. Soweto, she says, is cleaner and more organised than ever before. More streets are paved and lit and shiny, black-lettered street signs

117

have appeared on roads that had not borne names for years, if ever.

No place in Soweto has changed more than Orlando West, the Mecca of township tourism. Just blocks from Dolly's house is the former home of Nelson and Winnie Mandela and the Hector Petersen memorial, both obligatory stops on popular Soweto tours. Several small guest houses have opened, including her Dakalo Bed & Breakfast, along with new restaurants. Most of these eateries have been built for tourists, but a few are gaining popularity among locals too. One, which I visited for dinner, was swanky, stylish and filled with beautiful young blacks who had driven there in fancy cars.

It marked a contrast to my first visit to Orlando West soon after arriving in South Africa in January 2001. I took a Soweto tour and found the experience slightly distasteful. There was something voyeuristic and condescending about a group of rich foreigners being brought to speak to a *sangoma* (a traditional healer) in traditional skins. Orlando West on that first trip had that slightly artificial feeling that any place with too many tourists soon acquires.

This time, as the sun set and the tour buses headed home, I was seeing Soweto in a new light. I understood better why friends born there looked at it with nostalgia, even if they themselves have moved to the city. There is a community in Orlando West that my Johannesburg lacks and a deep sense of pride in its history and its role in the struggle.

But it is a somewhat forlorn nostalgia. Despite the tourists, Orlando West reminds me of an old company town dying because the industry that built it has left. Dolly and many of her neighbours are ageing and their children have moved to the city for work or school. I met one man who took his family to Soweto from Hillbrow after the 1994 elections, but he seemed to be the exception.

Most families who can afford it are moving out. The young generation, like Dolly's daughters, sees its future in the formerly forbidden northern neighbourhoods. They settle in places which their parents could only visit as domestic workers or gardeners. They come back at weekends or for the evening to patronise Soweto's bars and restaurants or its popular new nightclub The Rock, but their lives are elsewhere. AIDS, too, is stealing Soweto's young and Dolly says weekly funerals have replaced weddings as Soweto's major social functions. Death and exodus are taking their toll.

Nicole Itano is a freelance journalist, based in Johannesburg, who has written for various American media including the *Christian Science Monitor*, the *New York Times* and, most recently, the *Associated Press*.

Time to shine up

Aggrey Klaaste

There was a time – and for some of us this tendency continues – when journalists, writers, poets and artists of all types serenaded ghettos like Sophiatown and Soweto. This is not unique to South Africa because even slums like Harlem in New York were described in ways that said they were magical, swinging, upbeat.

South African ghettos were a creation of social engineering by racists, but this conurbation of townships did have a certain avant-garde mystique about it. Like the slums of Sophiatown and Harlem, the townships might be run-down, dirty, dangerous and uninhabitable but they have an unmistakable dance, sassiness and a beat about them. It is no wonder that the pint-sized ponytailed Sowetan girl who burst into a song that went *koloi ena ha ena mabili* – this car has no wheels – brought a smile quivering to my lips. This is part of the thing, part of the Soweto magic. As I am part of the furniture, and have lived here for more than half a century, I know the song. I know the code. I love it.

That is also why, when I entered my home and heard my son say *Ziya wa: ziwa more* – the party swings like hell – I felt at home. There is most certainly a swing and a dazzle about the lifestyle in the townships. But I know more, very much more.

I know the phoney magic of the shebeens. I know the heart-stopping crazy driving of black taxis. I know the drums of the Zion Church and have been dazzled by the incredible drumming of the *sangoma*. I know the love and the laughter and have lived through some of the worst tragedies and the greatest sadness.

I was there when the anger tore a swathe of bloody violence through all black townships after the Sharpeville massacre in 1960. The electrifying spirit of defiance and discovery inevitably caught me when Robert Sobukwe and other political leaders spoke of a different kind of black renaissance, Pan Africanism.

I was a close witness to the incredible explosion of anger in 1976 that led to protest poetry from people like Maishe Maponya, Don Mattera and Wally Serote. I was privileged to see the birth of the toyi-toyi. I was witness to the anger of beautiful young people who turned into monsters of death – the same children who had created lovely little parklands in the ghastly violence and dirt caused by the fight against apartheid.

One day I was in the streets of Soweto during the bloody battles – during which white and black policemen routinely shot everything that moved as they drove by – when I saw a group of neatly dressed schoolboys and girls. When asked where they were going they said they were going to kill a man. They didn't bat an eyelid. Later they hauled a man about, stabbed him with knives and what looked like garden forks. They literally cut him to pieces.

121

This was before the days of the dreaded 'necklace', which had the threatening ring of death and glamour. This was at the time when the dance of death, the toyi-toyi, was born. God only knows why it was given a sweet, almost childlike name. It was orchestrated and danced by schoolboys and girls who seemed to be in a grotesque trance as they trotted, chanting *hai-hai* in step. They'd place a tyre around the neck of some unfortunate devil, douse it with petrol and set it alight. You needed a very strong stomach to watch and to listen to the wails of a burning, helpless, ghastly human being. The architects of apartheid by accident or design created other forms of unbelievable conflict and death between blacks. They then called it black-on-black violence.

There were no Zulu male hostels in the days of Sofasonke Mpanza, one of the founders of Soweto. He was typically Sowetan. He ran several racehorses in the narrow streets of Orlando when it was illegal to own even a *spaza* shop, let alone a racehorse. But in 1956 Zulu male domestic workers who lived in the 'locations in the sky' – the domestic quarters on the roofs of high-rise flats which they cleaned – were moved to Soweto. They were moved into hostels that inevitably became the vortex of some of the most terrible violence that we lived through in Soweto.

Before then there was 'normal' crime and mayhem in Soweto. But these men, who were respectable married rural folk, with homes and families far away in the hills of Natal, were housed within the sassy, cheeky, 'disrespectful' townships of Soweto. Then the fuse was lit and explosions followed that almost tore out the heart of the township from 1976 into the late eighties.

Life was hell. At one time Mzimhlophe township, which was cheek by jowl with the Mzimhlophe Hostel, was razed almost to the ground and deserted after a war between the hostel and the township residents. Today, however, hostel dwellers live quite happily with township people.

Soweto is a metaphor for black life in South Africa. Even in unheard of places like Uitenhage in the Western Cape we discovered angry Soweto-type locations. The people behaved like township people in Soweto, in Mamelodi in Pretoria, in KwaMashu in Durban and Khayelitsha in Cape Town. The same beat. The same swing. The same cheek. The same deathly fury.

One of the more entrancing things about these places is the street or community song. In the days of apartheid there were songs about women, about Jozi, about shebeens, about white people and about the people's anger. They said, *Ons dak nie ons phola hier*, in the curious Afrikaans slang of Sophiatown, and I'm damned if that was not turned into a snappy ditty. There was even a song about tornadoes that were quite frequent. The people of Sophiatown and, later, the people of Orlando East and West, Pimville and Rockville in Soweto were deeply into jazz. You are more likely to hear kwaito music these days. Which is sad but fact.

Naturally nightlife is still exciting in Soweto. There are shebeens all over the townships and you are also likely to hear the music of Hugh Masekela played out in some rude, crude and huge loudness that has no thought for privacy. It is not disrespectful. It is just assumed that this is part of the life of the townships and no one ever calls the cops because of blaring noise.

Finally even the religion is colourful. There is a spray of green and red gowns every Sunday, the dress of both men and women, some men carrying white staves that are quite biblical. There are groups of men in long, pure white gowns blowing – what shall I call them? – huge bassoon-like instruments, doing some enchanting shuffle outside a hostel. They are members of the 'Shembe' church which is authentic Zulu Christian in garb and ceremony. Their worship is sombre, almost trance-like, a wonderful thing to see. Other churches are more animated. The Zion dance, which can get hypnotic even if you are just looking on, is typical of Sunday worship in the townships.

Is it worth it to stay in Soweto where a doctor who was fighting HIV/AIDS was shot dead while leaving his grandmother's grave at Doornkop Cemetery? Soweto and other Sowetos all over the country will not stay the way they are. They need to improve, to shine up. There is some brightening going on: in contrast to the days when it had only two traffic lights, Soweto is ablaze with all kinds of light today. But the modern-day businessperson must help turn the township into an elegant city and make Soweto the very heart of South Africa.

Aggrey Klaaste was editor-in-chief of the *Sowetan* when it was the country's largest circulation daily newspaper. He was the architect of its Nation Building campaign, which he still runs from the newspaper's corporate headquarters. He also worked for publications like *World*, *Drum*, *Post*, *Trust* and *Transvaal Post*.

A night with December

Mark Klusener

'Bring your *inyama*, bring your *utshwala*, bring your *izifebe*.'
Everyone roared with laughter, as I took another pull on the
Black Label beer which was being passed around in a jam jar.

'So you think our women are whores.' It was a statement,
not a question, and it came from the guy who had just joined
our group.

I looked up over the lip of my jar, and observed the speaker.
He was big, with a mean looking face. He had the look of a
person you didn't want to meet in a dark alley. He was a
definite 'don't mess with me' type of guy, and I had just
offended him.

'So you think our women are whores,' he repeated. I looked
around my group; it had all gone very quiet. Even the
youngsters washing our cars a short distance away had slipped
into silence, watching the situation unfold. It was the first
time in the three days of flat-out partying in Soweto that I

125

felt unsure of myself. It was the first time I noticed and felt like an intruder. I swallowed hard.

But before I could say anything the heavens opened and we rushed for cover. Clutching the beers we crammed underneath the overhang of an old, abandoned movie cinema. As luck would have it I was pushed up against the mean looking guy. He looked down at me.

I felt like a real idiot. I was being disrespectful. I knew I had no right calling anyone an *isifebe*. Actually I probably had no right even being here, what was I thinking, hanging out in the township? With growing discomfort I gave in, offering the last thing I had, the half-full Black Label. He took a long pull from the jar, smacked his lips, and took another drink. Then he looked down at me again.

'So what time is this party?'

'Eight o'clock,' I replied.

He nodded and walked out into the rain, towards his old Honda Civic. Without looking back he climbed in and drove off.

'Who the hell was that?' I asked.

'That was December, and he's a gangster,' somebody mumbled as they took another drag of a joint that was being passed around.

Nine hours later, the party was in full swing. Meat was sizzling on the grill, beers were flowing and, yes, the women were bumping and grinding to some local tunes. The party was at a colleague's house: his small garden was crammed with people, his house the same.

'Great party,' I shouted above the noise.

'Yeah. Hey, there is someone here to see you,' my friend said.

'Here, to see me? Who?' He didn't answer. He just waved his thumb in the general direction of the entrance.

I saw him almost immediately; he was hard to miss. Standing in a small group, he was looking directly at me.

December! I reluctantly moved over to the group.

'Hey guys, this is Mark and he thinks our women are whores,' he said by way of introduction.

There was silence for a few seconds, then one guy chipped in.

'But bru, our women *are* whores.'

Everyone burst out laughing. I looked over at December; tears were rolling down his cheeks as he laughed.

'Come on Mark, let's go,' he said and grabbed the beer from my hand. As we worked our way through the crowds he stopped to greet people. He introduced me.

'*Kuhamba kanjaan?*' I asked.

'So you speak Zulu?'

'Not very well, just the basics.'

He nodded and we carried on in silence.

'Where's your car?' he asked.

'It's over there, why?'

'That piece of shit, man, I could steal that in twenty seconds.'

'It's got a gearlock and immobiliser, no way you can steal that in twenty seconds.'

'Ten bucks says I can.' He smiled as I nodded.

It actually took him thirty seconds to have my car out of the driveway, but he was using one hand as the other determinedly held on to his beer.

He took the car around the block and brought it back.

'Hey, let's go for a ride,' he said as he tossed me the keys to his car.

As we drove through the streets of Protea Glen, I asked for directions.

'Zola.'

Just the mention of that area made me nervous. It was after eleven o'clock at night and I was driving around with somebody who could steal a car in seconds. And we were heading into the most notorious area of Soweto. Great move. But I said nothing. If I was going to die tonight it was as good a night as any, I suppose.

December didn't speak much, except to give me directions.

'Stop here,' he said on a poorly lit street.

He wound down the window and called out softly to a stranger lurking in the shadows. An old man emerged and climbed into the car. He nodded his head in greeting to me and we drove on. Ten minutes later December again told me to stop. The old man got out of the car, thanked us and carried on walking.

'Nice guy,' I said by way of breaking the silence.

'Not really, he used to be a professional soccer coach, now he kills people for money,' replied December matter of factly.

Five minutes later we stopped outside a small house. It looked vaguely familiar.

'We've driven past it three times, just checking,' December said.

'Who lives here, another contract killer?'

He knocked on the door and a few moments later a woman opened up. She didn't say much, and didn't look at all surprised to see a white man standing at her door at this time of night.

'Come in,' December said.

He spoke rapidly to the woman in Sesotho. She disappeared and a few minutes later emerged with a small boy, about five or six years old. The child rubbed his eyes then let out a squeal of joy as he ran to December.

'This is my boy,' he said with pride, hoisting the child up in the air and giving him a hug. The child cuddled up to his father and eventually looked up at me with big eyes.

'Say hello to the *mlungu*,' he told the child.

'Hello *mlungu*,' the boy said, then hid his face in his father's jacket.

We sat for a few minutes. Father and son saying nothing. After a while the child's breathing became deeper and when he gave a little snore December handed him back to his mother.

'Let's go,' he said and he rose.

As we walked back to the car, he turned to me.

'They may be whores, but that is their gift to us.'

Mark Klusener is a journalist working at South Africa's independent television station e.tv. He has spent over ten years working in print, radio and television. He lived in Soweto for a short time, and now lives in Johannesburg.

Wrestling

James Lamont

It took Mike almost two years to tell me who he was. The man responsible for our undisturbed sleep, it turned out, was a Zimbabwean. He lived in Soweto as one of millions of Zimbabweans making South Africa their home. Many found casual employment as guards, gardeners and farmhands; the more skilled got better paid jobs in banks, hospitals and universities.

Mike Nkosi was a nightwatchman, a security guard, with a wife, two children and a monthly salary of a little more than 1 800 rand. He worked a twelve-hour shift and returned to Soweto at dawn.

Seeing out his nightly vigil in a greatcoat and balaclava, he was one of a gathering number of economic refugees from the crisis engulfing his country under President Robert Mugabe. Although overqualified for his job, he had a resilient good humour about his predicament. He had an income, easy access to food and, generally, a more predictable life than back home.

But until the day he nervously disclosed his origins – almost as if expecting an instant diminution – his identity was obscure. He had said he was from Benoni, on the East Rand, with a connection to Mpumalanga. An uncle lived somewhere nearby. He was, he first told me, Ndebele and held South African papers. He lived in Soweto.

Johannesburg lends itself to those who seek to reinvent their lives. It offers a modest African equivalent to the American dream. So scant information exchanged over cups of tea easily passes as the bare bones of friendship. Not many questions, not many lies. Mike had aspirations to be a teacher. But he had worked in a dry-cleaning shop. Then he found himself as my night guard, armed against burglars with a radio sporting a coat-hanger aerial and the Bible. He was a fragile replacement for a regiment of silent, weapon-toting Namibian security men, who had disgraced themselves by shooting a hole in my landlord's roof.

But Mike invited curiosity. His avid reading struck me first. He was religious. His companion through the night was his heavily hand-annotated Bible. He had a distant ambition to go to Bible college. And he could speak beginner's Portuguese, words of which we exchanged in brief cellphone conversations. Then there was his attachment to England. He made a request for an Oxford University sweatshirt when a friend visited. He called his daughter Ebeneezer, not knowing the reference to Scrooge of Charles Dickens' *A Christmas Carol*.

Then, not long after letting me into the secret of his nationality, Mike invited my wife and me to his Zimbabwean church: a billowing tarpaulin-covered warehouse in Hillbrow. After that came an invitation to his home in Soweto.

My knowledge of Soweto was a bit like my knowledge of Mike: I just had the basic facts. These were pinned loosely to the political history books. There was Regina Mundi church, the cemetery, the Hector Petersen museum and Winnie Mandela's house. I had watched a match at the Soweto Cricket Oval. I'd talked to despairing nurses in the Intensive Care Unit of Chris Hani Baragwanath Hospital, attended a wedding of a colleague and made a quick exit from a post-football match party after a car was set alight. I had also watched an HIV/AIDS performance with the grandees of Sophiatown at Mrs Motlana's house – the wife of Nthato Motlana, doctor to Nelson Mandela. It always seemed to rain there. But mostly Soweto appeared to be a big place in which a visitor could very easily get lost.

Mike was not going to leave anything to chance. So he intercepted us at a traffic light not far from the Moroka police station. It was a short journey to where he lived, beyond a brightly coloured bar. A wedding was under way a couple of doors down and guests were beginning to drift away when we arrived in his street.

Mike stayed with a landlady, an old woman who had connections – a deceased husband – to Zimbabwe. The yard was meticulously swept like a rural tenement. Mike, his wife Chipo, and his two children, had a small room in an outhouse with a bed partitioned off from a tiny kitchen. There was no ceiling, just a sloping corrugated iron roof.

We were ushered into the main four-roomed house and sat in a neat dining room, bathed in a half-light that struggled through heavy net curtains. We admired Ebeneezer. Out came generous servings of tea, biscuits and French toast. The room swelled with curious children. And on went a big screen television in the corner. The World Wrestling Federation, a pantomime of Western culture, beamed itself into this hospitable corner of Africa as an oblique tribute to the world where we were from.

Big men in leotards and wearing wrist thongs on their forearms growled at each other. They wrestled against the ropes and stamped on each other's torsos. Then they turned

132

their attentions to a woman wrestler, hurling accusations that she was a lesbian. The crowd booed. Torches of flame flared. New burly contestants replaced Gold Dust and The Undertaker.

The children in the room were utterly transfixed. WWF's bizarre theatre was favourite Sunday afternoon viewing. The wrestlers were household names. Conversation was stifled.

The WWF's mock violence and diabolical styling made me uneasy. I have heard Fidel Castro, the president of Cuba, and other leaders tell how Tarzan films moulded their misunderstanding of Africa. The antics of the bellowing, tree-swooping hero of their youth conjured up a world of impenetrable jungle, cannibals dancing round cooking pots and silent assassins with lethal blowpipes.

Was WWF any different in communicating a distorted image of the West to young people in Soweto? When they encountered me and my North American wife did WWF join David Beckham, the Queen and wealth as their associations with my world? I could see it fermenting rage among those a little older, a little more zealous, among those who might fear their delicate, ascetic cultures being crushed by a brute world power. I wondered about their reactions; might they rebel against it, or fight it?

WWF scared me, much more than Soweto did. Mike was embarrassed about where he was from. His prosperity and ambitions had been wrestled to the ground by greed and misrule. But, that day, I shared his blushes.

James Lamont was the *Financial Times* southern Africa bureau chief until 2003. He lived and worked in South Africa for several years, including four years as editor of the daily paper *Business Report*. He now lives in London, with his wife and young son, where he works for the *Financial Times*.

133

Da Revulsion won't be televised: Fighting for the right to funk it up

Bongani Madondo

Bet you've seen 'em 'round your local mall – where else? – clad in parachute-sized jeans and necks weighed down with thick gold chains straight out of that anti-slavery film epic, *Sankofa*. The boys walk with an almost choreographed gait, what Tom Wolfe has referred to as the 'pimp roll'; their all too supple girls, called 'fly gals' when they toe the line, 'bitches and hos' when they don't, are identified by their nouveau-Afro tank tops: *aaaamandla*! Radicals they may be, but these boys are at home bump 'n' grinding their way around marbled-floor malls in the latest Nike sneakers. The names Arundhati Roy and Naomi Klein sound like new 4x4s to them. No Logo? What? You won't find no mobile human billboards like these teens.

Well, if your scope of young blacks in the post-freedom

era veers only as far as the NBBPs, or New Black Brat Packs, then you have not even begun scratching the surface of that perennially desperate question: 'where is the black youth?' To answer it, you have to foot it to the townships, specifically Soweto's much-romanticised dusty streets, still the bedrock of urban youth angst. These streets are the midwives of a new, cynical, feisty, rap-inspired Afro-revolutionary vanguard, an artistic and political cultural movement known simply as 'Black Sunday'.

Black Sunday is a Soweto-born black 'n' proud youth movement that takes place every Sunday in diverse areas of the township such as Diepkloof, Naledi and Meadowlands. From a distance this might just qualify as the freshest thing since the seventies' Staff Rider and Classic's black beat Afro-jazzed poets. But Black Sunday is as underground a movement as London's Blacktronica or Soweto's bygone Medupe: assertive and proud.

Black Sunday members inhabit a world of their own. They want a 'new Africa', one that connects the supreme spirit of John Coltrane, a hip quota of the guitar gods Carlos Santana and Jimi Hendrix, and historical African figures such as vhaVenda Paramount King Makhado, Zulu icon Shaka and Basotho's feminist Queen Manthatise.

Take a stroll down the main road branching off Old Potch Road that leads to the Chris Hani Baragwanath Hospital, down to Diepkloof's Zone 5 on any Sunday afternoon. Before long, amid the throngs of township dwellers – Pentecostal church-going grannies; Irish linen-suited 4x4 black elites zig-zagging back to suburbia after an hour with 'mom' in the 'hoods' – your eardrums are bombarded by a crackling cry or by scattergun lyrics piped into the open air by loudspeakers.

Once I made my way to the centre of a hidden recreational square, *laagered* by a rusty barbed wire fence where the peak point of new black artistic radical angst is at. You've heard the sound miles away. Now your eyes are met by a gathering of hundreds if not thousands of black teenagers milling around.

As Common Man, one of Black Sunday's superbrains and poet laureate put it, their 'identity' separates them from the 'mainstream black demographic'. How? They aren't talking. You are invited to 'experience it'.

'It's located deep in the type of music and politics we try to create. Deep in that fibre, you check?' clarifies DJ Hempza, a father figure and one of the main organisers.

Also, they'll tell you, it's all about 'feeling; deeper feelings'. Which is nothing like the celebrity tear fest hawked on Oprah or sad feelings that lie lingering on Hollywood stars waiting for the Dalai Lama's magic wand. Nope.

'Deep feelings' for them, is nothing like Jeff Buckley, Eric Clapton or even Lauryn Hill's blues. This is rather a yearning for a National Geographic Africa of yore to merge with a high-tech African space they now occupy.

Now a variety of poets chant and rap along to a backdrop of multi-bass beats stored and clicked from Windows 2000 computers, MP3s and turntables, all connected by electricity stolen from the nearby community church. Nkosi, sikelele I' A*free*kah, indeed. 'Afro-coexistence you see?' Hempza urges me. I don't bite it, but of course I'm smitten by the Do-It-Yourself sensibilities at play here.

Soon, it becomes clear that the terms 'microchip' and 'umqusho' are both part of an edgy, refashioned lingua franca amongst these youth. Some speak in a mangled, yet musically tilting New Age fanagalo that combines isiZulu, seTswana and American ebonics all wrapped into a rap lingo that is, you realise, a dialect understood by the cultural sect alone.

The poets – who are received as street prophets if they are good and as dispensable trash if they aren't – are greeted with collective screams: *'mo' faya. Umlilo! mo-faa-ya . . .'*

'Mo' faya', slang for 'go ahead raise the stakes', is part of a Rasta and hip-hop lingo meant to encourage and inspire the

self-proclaimed warrior-poets to tap into their genius. That's if there's any.

And there's the story of the dress code, the easiest reflection of the cultural revisionism at play here. The movement's young girls, often referred to as 'Queens', are attired in ankle-touching, flowing skirts and a variety of long, back-sliding headgears, gold and copper fields of bangles and some huge Egyptian accessories for good measure. Intrigued, I approach one of the Queens to check how their Queenness gets to mix with such a misogynistic art form as rap.

'My name is Tutan,' the young lady in an orange skirt says. 'Tutankhamun, queen of the sun,' she introduces herself, but she couldn't maintain the oh-so cordial African veneer for long.

'Sorry sisi,' I tell her. 'You can't possibly be Tutankhamun. That was a pharaoh boy king, Akhenaten's heir, wasn't it? And wasn't somebody called Osiris the actual queen of the sun, no?'

She fires back: 'I choose who I want to be. *Wena uwubani?*'

Dead icons they also hold in reverence: Bob Marley, Steve Biko and rapper Talib Kweli make the holy trinity of deities. Having a slight insight into Peter Tosh's lyrics makes you cooler than poring over Nelson Mandela's *Long Walk To Freedom* among the Black Sundayers. If not seen as a New Age drama king, the old man has sadly become fodder for jokes: 'I mean he's Naomi Campbell's friend, right?' another teen girl with an Egyptian-sounding name laughs.

One boy choruses: 'Yebo! Which makes him King of the Queens.' He gesticulates, self-satisfied with his wit 'n' irony all rolled in one. 'Yeah. You should see him in famous photographs. Ol'man is King of the Queens. With Naomi this side and David Beckham on the other side, Madiba really rocks, weee-ho ho ho,' they all join in the punchline.

Talent and variety abound in these dusty streets. Within this 'tribe' an array of alternative artists like hip-hop photographers, spin-deejays, self-taught computer programmers exist cheek by jowl with amateur home videographers and Afro-bead designers. 'Do-it-yourself' is the big racket – oops – spiritual mantra here.

Like post-independent revolutionaries anywhere, language is a hot political potato. Says chief organiser Hempza, 'We call our rappers *izimbongi* and only chronicle our stories in Zulu and other indigenous dialects. Don't give us this rubbish American and private school accents.'

They see themselves as the vanguard of a future Africa, a romantic Africa that can be mouse clicked into new technology without upsetting its romance, history, *amasiko* . . .

But on close inspection, these new Africanists with their seTswana and isiZulu sonic vignettes and scattergun rhyming, sound exactly like the self-praising maskanda artists and elderly traditional village folk who rap of nothing else but conquering the enemy. And like maskanda stars such as Ukhansela, the late Mfazi O'Mnyama and uTwalufu, these rappers' lyrics are saturated with self-praise, their place of origins and family trees. And how the singers pride themselves on their male prowess.

As an art they are pure rap, as a lifestyle they are hip-hop, but as a cultural movement their expression aspires to the ancient Zulu, baKone, vhaVenda and other African national-ities whose menfolk would pride themselves on their hunting skills, pelvic power, the number of enemies they've slain and, the priciest, acquired cattle and women.

Spending a day with them, it became clear that though accusations of 'lost generation' are far-fetched, there is an unmistakable loss of innocence and a sadness here. African parents in the ecstatic throes of early nineties Mandelamania, the glossy black empowered middle class and their stinking poor counterparts, have abdicated parental responsibilities. They've given them over to parental advisory stickers, MTV and malls. So the new generation is out of sync and out of sight.

Those home during news hours watch with feigned revulsion as their children drown in drug pools or play stick-ups with real rods, 38s, Baby Brown, *whacha* want, only fifty rand and you are boss of the road gaz' lam.

What could the adults do? They might try to connect through music. Adults could do well to revisit the genesis of *Kwela* music, way back in Sophiatown. It was *Kwela* – with Aaron Lerole, Spokes Mashiane and Lemmy Special Mabaso hot on the pennywhistle – in Sophiatown that reflected black youth's disgust at the oppressive Afrikaner regime, black adults' conservatism and America's big jazz band imperialism. Just as *Kwela* was politics, these Black Sundayers with their well-defined African nationalist pride are political too.

'The thing is, our politics are not theirs,' says rapper Ngwenya, one of the movement's products and possibly one of the most gifted black pop impressionists to come out of South African youth culture.

But it may not be so different. *Kwela* had a powerful yet temporary reign in the fifties, and now its era is nostagically spoken of as a golden time for urban black youth's cultural zenith; a reflection of a deeply felt yearning for pure, defiant fun. Today in Diepkloof's noisy, high-spirited streets one has a gut feeling that these young Sowetans are today's new-tech Afro-radicals.

The computer mouse is in sight. Click!

A self-confessed country bumpkin, Bongani Madondo is a features writer at the *Sunday Times* who has a love-hate relationship with Soweto. He is also a published essayist and Arts and Culture Journalist of 2003-2004. This is a reworked version of an article that first appeared in the *Sunday Times* (*Lifestyle section*) in October 2003.

Bomvana

Mongadi Mafata

Grey hair peeps out from under the green and black *doek* that Orlando East resident Ruth Bomvana is wearing. She says her introduction to Orlando East, the second oldest suburb in Soweto, was heart-wrenching and unforgettable. Bomvana's family were among the black residents of the former Malay Camp outside the Johannesburg city centre who were forcibly removed to make way for Indians. Hundreds of black people like her were forced to abandon friends and schoolmates as they were loaded onto Johannesburg city council trucks with their belongings and relocated to Orlando East, about thirty kilometres from the city.

The year was 1937, five years after the birth of Orlando East when the whites-only parliament decreed that pockets of multiracial residential areas dotting South Africa's major cities were to be purged of black residents. Bomvana, who was fourteen years old at the time, and her family were made to squeeze into a two-roomed council house and ordered to pay 14 shillings and 4 pence to the council.

'The streets were not tarred. We had to share a communal tap down the street and *bo-ntate tshutsha* – night soil removers – would come in the evenings on carts pulled by oxen,' Bomvana says as she fiddles with her spectacles. She laughs as she relates how children used to be scared witless at the mere mention of *ntate tshutsha*. 'When mothers wanted to stop children from crying, they would just tell them that *ntate tshutsha* was coming.'

Bomvana says nurses of that era were fit. They had to be. 'Most of the nurses were midwives and they used to cycle around the township and help pregnant women deliver babies in their homes. Unlike now when babies are delivered in hospitals, babies were delivered in their homes.'

Crime was unheard of. Men organised themselves into neighbourhood watches and *tsotsis*, who preyed on the newly arrived country bumpkins, were dealt with very swiftly. But, the same strong men who meted out instant punishment to *tsotsis* cowered when the dreaded Black Jacks – the notorious council policemen – banged on doors to check whether residential permits were in order.

'They would knock on the doors and shout: "*Gqoka sihambe*" – get dressed and come with us – if your permit had expired. It was very humiliating for the black man. Those who had just come from the rural areas and had not registered with the council as residents, would be trooped to the police station to spend the night there,' Bomvana says.

Bomvana also tells of Redifusion, a radio service designed to keep the natives docile. It beamed government propaganda and nearly every house in Orlando East had little box speakers wired to it.

'Most residents hated *msakazo* but there was no affordable alternative,' Bomvana says.

Apartheid's grand plan was for blacks to serve whites in

141

the cities and when they couldn't do that they had to retire to Bantustan homelands. Orlando East residents had other ideas. They defied the restrictive by-laws that prevented them from extending their tiny houses. Sense finally prevailed and those who could afford it turned their houses into comfortable living spaces.

Another way to 'keep the natives happy' was to build them beerhalls dotted all over the sprawling township. Only sorghum beer was sold at the beerhalls. The men, only men were allowed into the beerhalls, sat on long benches, with their containers of beer at their feet. They would occasionally lift the beer to their lips, pass the 'scale' to their neighbours and wipe their lips with the backs of their hands. This was the place they exchanged tales of their woes in the white man's city.

'It's not surprising that the first thing that our children did when they revolted against Bantu Education and Afrikaans being thrust down their throats in 1976 was to tear down all the beerhalls.

'They said that their fathers spent their wages on booze and returned home with sob stories about how they were robbed on their way home,' Bomvana chuckles. The only tarred roads then were the ones that led to the beerhalls so that council trucks that delivered the beer wouldn't get stuck on gravel pathways that snaked throughout the townships.

Bomvana, a member of the local Catholic parish, is proud that while all other mission schools buckled under government pressure to convert to public schools under the Department of Bantu Education, the Roman Catholic Church successfully resisted. 'We fought with the Nationalist government which wanted to water down our children's education when they introduced Bantu Education in the 1950s,' Bomvana says.

The Methodist, Anglican, Baptist and Salvation Army schools gave in to the government's demands rather than continue without subsidies. Bomvana, who was among the first black matrons at Chris Hani Baragwanath Hospital and was married to a local schoolteacher, elected to send her son Thamsanqa to school in Swaziland. Thamsanqa is now district surgeon in Soweto.

Despite sometimes cruel methods to keep blacks from mainstream politics, voices of dissent gathered momentum. One was that of the late African National Congress stalwart, Walter Sisulu, once a resident of Orlando East. He and others such as former President Nelson Mandela and the late Anton Lembede, who were members of the ANC Youth League, agitated for change. Lembede, who was uncomfortable with whites being at the helm of the people's struggle, influenced a breakaway group that formed the Pan Africanist Congress of Azania in Orlando East's Communal Hall in 1959.

It's been seventy-two years since Orlando East was established and ten years into democracy some of the roads in the township are still not tarred. Unemployment and a lack of business opportunities have forced many Orlando East residents to cram corrugated iron shacks into their yards to supplement their incomes from renting the dwellings. For Bomvana and thousands like her in the township, the struggle continues.

Mongadi Mafata joined the *Sowetan* in 1994, is now the news editor and is 'passionate about preserving black people's history'.

Mother and daughter

Pearl Majola

My mother Dumazile Margaret Majola is a good storyteller. She can have you in stitches telling a simple story about burial society scams and other goings-on at the pension payout point of Magabheni, a small township hidden behind the plush coastal suburbs of Umkomaas, south of Durban. And she can just as easily have you mesmerised with the mysterious stories of *abathakathi* (witches) of Bhekithemba (now known as Umlazi township), where she was born some seventy years ago, *izipoki* (ghosts) of King Edward Hospital, where she studied nursing administration, or the very real horrors of the violence that gripped KwaZulu-Natal in the eighties and early nineties.

I recently visited my mother and she told me, ten years after she retired, about the beginning of her nursing career in the early fifties. She shared a compartment on the train from Durban with three Zimbabwean ladies who arranged for their boyfriends to take her to the bus from Park Station to Johannesburg General, where she and other new recruits would be received before proceeding to Baragwanath Hospital in Soweto.

My mother told me what sounded like a story of young conscripts arriving at an army camp, how on the first day they were received by an official who showed them to yet another bus that would transport them to Bara from Jo'burg Gen, how they arrived at Bara, took tea, received their standard issue uniforms. The following day training began in earnest with how to make a bed.

She never really liked Soweto because of the *tsotsis* and *abeSotho* carrying on in seSotho as if they were the cleverest people that ever lived. As if it had happened just yesterday, she also told me of one incident that moved her and showed her the gentle side of *abeSotho*, the *tsotsis* and Soweto amid all the callousness she experienced.

One Sunday morning she got on a bus on her way to church in Orlando. The bus was empty but for a gang of *tsotsis* sitting at the back. Naturally she sat in the front of the bus. But, as could be expected, they taunted her and eventually one of them approached her, saying the boss wanted to know who she was, where she was from, where she was going, and so on. She answered all the questions and the guy went back to report to the boss. On hearing this, the boss himself went over to my mother and told everyone to stop and listen. She was not to be harmed. She was to be looked after and she was to be escorted from the bus stop to the church.

It turned out that the young man had been a student at Amanzimtoti College near Durban and had found himself stranded in the area when the college expelled students and closed down to suppress a strike. Far from home and without money to board the train, he wandered about until a woman from the neighbourhood took him into her home, where he was looked after, helped to contact his parents and waited for weeks until money arrived to buy a train ticket.

When I announced about twelve years ago that I had been

offered a job on the *Sowetan* newspaper and that I would stay with my good friend Phangisile, my mother showed no signs of concern for her last-born child leaving home to make a new life in Johannesburg.

But the day I left, she warned me to avoid going to Soweto and if I couldn't, then I should not set foot in Orlando – it was dangerous, there were *tsotsis* everywhere, they could rob you in broad daylight. It was dangerous, she repeated herself.

Being the good child that I was, I took my mother's warning quite seriously and resolved to heed it – typical of a person who does not know Soweto. The reality was this: I was going to work for the *Sowetan*, a newspaper whose major circulation and readership are in Soweto. Orlando is where Mandela had lived. Winnie Mandela still lives in Orlando. Orlando Stadium was not only the home ground of my favourite team, Orlando Pirates, but also the venue for music festivals, political rallies, and more. The best *skobho* (cooked head of a sheep) I ever tasted was sold in Orlando. The house of my colleague Vusi was in Orlando. One of my contacts, Fikile, was based near Orlando. My homeboy and friend, Lu, lived there. Sharing a carpool with a colleague made it near impossible to avoid Orlando. How could I not set foot in Orlando?

I do not remember why I went there the first time, who I was with or what the work purpose of my visit was. I remember this though: I had to go at short notice. I thought of calling my mother but realised it was a bad idea – I had work to do and my mother had little to do with it. I was not afraid but have to admit I was a little apprehensive, especially because I could not quite share my anxiety or explain it to my colleagues. I was also uneasy because I had observed that my colleagues, the drivers, tended to speak fluent Afrikaans, seSotho and seTswana instead of English, whereas my language skills then were limited to a lot of isiZulu, English and some isiXhosa. If anything happened, how would I cope?

But nothing happened: we could have been in the neighbourhood where I grew up. People, who spoke mainly isiZulu, went about their business as they do in any other township. Yes, it was big. There were robots everywhere, and for this Jane comes to Jo'burg, robots in a township were a big thing. This was a city, not a township. No one looked like a *tsotsi,* though it is not as if they are branded. No one was robbed while I was there. I felt perfectly safe.

My mother knows now that I have been to Soweto many times. A few years ago I took her to my aunt (her sister-in-law) in Chiawelo – the first time she has been back since she left Soweto in the fifties. As we drove past Bara, she remarked that it had changed. Of course it would have, she seemed to correct herself. It was busier, she noted. The entrance hadn't changed much. What would it be like inside, she wondered out loud. Would she like to go in and look around, I asked. No, she said emphatically.

I have lived in Johannesburg for many years, but in my limited experience of Soweto I have found it quite different from what I first imagined. In shebeens at night, guys who look like any other ordinary black man have bought me a drink of my choice and chatted me up as expected, but I have felt as safe, if not safer, as I have sitting on the pavement part of a restaurant at The Zone in Rosebank on a Saturday afternoon.

Now and then I hang out at my friend's payphone shop in Mofolo where I can't help but overhear fellow migrant workers, usually from the Eastern Cape or KwaZulu-Natal, running their homes by remote; love-struck youngsters making love on the phone; lovers breaking up; and, once, a young man explaining to a voice on the other side that he did not have medical aid but had cash and the ambulance should come immediately because his mother desperately needed medical attention.

I have seen sheer grit and entrepreneurship in Soweto: unassuming women selling *skobho, mala mogodu* and other offal, fanning away the flies all the while; the mechanic running a workshop on the side of the road; a world-renowned restaurant that will hold its own among the best in the country; as well as the chutzpah and lightning speed of the *tsotsis* that held up my friend at gunpoint and took all the computers, faxes, phones, microwave and other valuables from her shop in three minutes.

I have seen an amazing resilience in Soweto: a hospice; people standing in the sweltering heat in a dusty graveyard to bury loved ones; permanent potholes and smelly water puddles on the road; *Mshenguville*; the smothering smell of coal in the early winter afternoons and the brown-black donkeys lugging coal on a grim winter's day.

I have also seen colours as bright as your imagination will allow: shining red or green stoeps and the smallest and neatest lawns in people's yards; snazzy gay people strutting their stuff as if there were no tomorrow; vibrant murals and graffiti on the walls fencing off institutions alongside main roads; Zionists in sparkling white, green and blue garb walking to an all night prayer meeting on Saturday; lavish weddings for which whole streets get closed off; old ladies my mother's age, getting down to the sounds of Mafikizolo's '*Kugug othandayo*'; black men in check pants and funny shoes teeing off on a well-tended green; amaVenda, abeLungu and other colourful people everywhere, speaking all the eleven official languages plus one, *tsotsitaal*.

Did my mother lie about Soweto? No. I think she had a different experience at a different time. I have never personally witnessed crime or violence in Soweto, never felt any fear, exclusion, being out of place or unwelcome there. Now and then people have commented on my heavy Zulu accent, which I am proud of so I don't mind the comments. I can't say I particularly like it because generally I am intimidated by big cities, but Soweto sure fascinates and inspires me at the same time. *Kuyashesha lapha*!

Pearl Majola worked for the *Sowetan*. She is now an executive in a cellphone company.

148

Dube Boxing Club

Stéphane Mayoux

It is the summer of 1998. With a clicking noise, skipping ropes flick the dusty floor of the bare room that is Dube Boxing Club, in Soweto. It is late afternoon. Particles of dust dance away from the ropes and stick to the heavy tongue of the old boxing trainer. He is barking numbers at three young men doing press-ups, chests in pain, open-mouthed, eyes to the ground. '25, 26, 27, 28, 29, 30. STOP!' And they stop, with wrinkled brows, the air barely hanging from their mouths, sweat dropping from their noses.

The old man shouts, waving a crooked finger. 'This one is a fief. Yes, you are a fief. Look at him! He's a fief, yeah . . . yeah. A fief.' The 'thief' steals a moment of rest. More young men enter the room. They won't box yet. They have to feel some real pain first. Maybe they won't box at all today. The old man giggles into his sweat – and starts counting again.

Dube Boxing Club is not a gym, it's just a dusty, covered

149

square in Soweto, packed full of sweaty dreams. The earth outside the gym is rough, with a few patches of grass. The room has hardly any windows. There's no ring, but a couple of heavy bags hang from the ceiling. Most weekdays, in the evening, young men come here to box, to hope and to pray. They assemble like disciples, their eyes intense. They smile the smiles of believers. Well, someone has given them reason to believe.

'Baby Jake' Matlala – surely the shortest man in boxing – local hero, living legend and four times world junior flyweight champion, has been working out in Dube for many years. He took the barking and the pain and the dust that propelled him to fame; and to the BMW parked outside the gym. He may be little, but he won big and, from time to time, 'Baby Jake' comes back to Dube Boxing Club to train with the crowd of young hopefuls.

Soon, the room is full. A different trainer now leads the drill. He too used to come to Dube as a young man. His workout is furiously loud. The room seems too small for all the shouting and all the exercise. Shoes hit the floor, fists beat the air, heads try to shake away the pain. The trainer's voice is counting down the evening. The dust has disappeared, but it's still in the lungs, in the ears. There is a military air to the exercise, a sense of common purpose and discipline that, on some nights, might just 'sweeten' life as it's known outside the gym in Soweto.

Within the walls of Dube Boxing Club there is certainty and shared rules and ambitions. The drill works itself up into a dance, then the men break up. There are jokes and smiles, and suddenly less noise. Time for punches: 'Box! Box!' On the wall a few paper cuttings give the results of the latest fights. Not all the Dube men and boys have done well.

In a corner, 'Baby Jake' goes through his paces with the old trainer. It is more a cuddle than a fight really. These steps and hooks have been rehearsed many times, like traditional,

150

local greetings. Other boxers practise in the opposite corner.

The workout is coming to a close. One of the trainers hands over to a teenager for the end-of-session prayer. 'Don't worry. It's yours. Go ahead.' The young man looks at a stranger in the room, turns his gaze to the floor and starts leading the prayer. He expresses thanks for the day's food and joys, for the day's work. Dube Boxing Club is silent for a while, no more punches through leather gloves, no more skipping ropes and painful chests. Everyone is slowly recovering their breath.

'. . . we thank you God! Amen.'
'Amen.'

But the old trainer wants a little bit more and pulls two youths out of the corner, shouting once more. 'Box! Box!'

In 1998, Dube Boxing Club was looking for funds for refurbishment, to become a real sports and boxing centre, they told me. When I visited the area a few years later, it seemed Dube had found the funds it had dared to hope for.

Stéphane Mayoux was born in Toulouse, in the south of France in 1967. He has worked with the BBC World Service since 1994, reporting on and from Africa and training journalists all over the continent. He lived in Jo'burg from 1998 to 2000, where he and his wife had their middle child Ophélie Naledi. Naledi (which means star in sesotho) is very proud of the fact.

Through my parents' eyes

Nokuthula Mazibuko

My father's earliest memories of Soweto are from the age of ten when he moved to live with his aunt in Albertinesville. His mother was struggling with six children, so she asked her sister to lend a hand. At that time, in 1953, the south-western townships were not known as Soweto and consisted mainly of the shack town Albertinesville and small brick houses in Pimville and Orlando. My father registered at the Catholic primary school St Matthews, one hundred kilometres from his family in KwaThema, Springs. He walked about five kilometres every day to reach St Matthews from Albertinesville and witnessed the myriad of indignities suffered by adults.

Daily he saw grown men run pathetically from white policemen who, barely out of their teens, demanded the dreaded passbook. The apartheid system required everyone over sixteen years of age to carry a pass; it was an attempt to control with rigour, impunity and violence the movements of blacks. The sight of poverty was everywhere, unemployment was rife, and men drowned their misery with liquor in illegal shebeens, and later in government-sponsored beerhalls.

My father's aunt made a precarious living washing white people's clothes. She would ask him to fetch the clothes in town on weekends, and then take them back washed, dried and ironed. On these trips to town he particularly noticed how beautiful and well-organised the schools were. He wondered why the white schools were much better than the black schools. His teacher and mentor Mr Drake Koka explained that Bantu Education was inferior and aimed to train them to be labourers.

Years later, in 1966, my father became a teacher himself, at the historic Morris Isaacson High where the anti-Bantu Education students uprising of 1976 started. His return to Soweto, after several years away, was the beginning of a life that centred on education and politics. Morris Isaacson was extremely dilapidated: the education ministry had ordered that black schools get just a fifth of the funding given to white schools. The school looked run down, but the teachers and the principal, Mr Lawrence Legau Mathabathe, were dedicated. Teachers encouraged political debate and involvement; they defied authorities by employing activist Onkgopotse Tiro who had been expelled from the University of the North for political activism. The authorities refused to pay Tiro's salary, so Mathabathe mobilised students and parents to raise funds for him through music concerts and by showing movies at the school.

A year after the 1976 riots in Soweto, teachers, through the Teachers' Action Committee, resigned en masse to protest against the murder of children by police and the continuing harassment of teachers. They drafted a common letter of resignation and collected 703 signed letters from teachers, which were delivered to the regional education office in Johannesburg. A month later, at four o'clock in the morning,

153

police conducted a simultaneous arrest of those behind the mass resignation. Many of them, including my father, spent the next year in prison.

After his release in 1978, the teachers continued speaking against apartheid and Bantu Education. My father got a banning order for his troubles; that stopped him leaving Johannesburg and ordered that he not be in the company of more than two people at any one time. At least he took this forced isolation as a chance to study and get a bachelor of science degree at Wits University.

Despite his tumultuous life, my father continued to work in education, raising funds for science and maths students after his banning order was lifted. He also met and married my mother, Miriam Mazibuko, and had three children. They met in Zululand, but managed to 'cook' their passes to be able to live together in Soweto, though legally they could only live, separately, in remote, rural parts of the country. Blacks were only allowed into the cities to work in white towns. If they had no employment they were to go back to their rural 'homelands'.

My mother is also a product of Soweto in many ways. She came to the township to complete high school at Orlando West High and lived in Diepkloof Zone 6. After getting her diploma, she worked at the department of Bantu Affairs as a probation officer. She worked with juvenile delinquents, investigating the circumstances that led youngsters to commit crimes, meeting families, neighbours and teachers. Her job brought her face to face with the worst of apartheid: abject poverty and extreme social dysfunction. She visited tiny homes with as many as twenty people living in them. She saw people overwhelmed by their poverty. She helped to rehabilitate delinquents who today are employed and have functioning families.

My parents now look at their lives in Soweto with wonder, not quite sure how they survived apartheid. They appreciate the light of day brought about by South Africa's democracy as a sharp contrast to the harrowing night when they did not know if they would survive, or what would become of their children. Now kids half their age hold jobs they never thought possible for a black person. Everyone has an equal chance to benefit from government institutions like schools, hospitals and welfare. Everyone has a right to live where they want to live.

Nokuthula Mazibuko is a writer based in Jo'burg. She plies her trade for educational TV and radio shows. She has also worked as a news producer for the BBC and the youth station Yfm. She is a PhD student at the Wits School of African Literature.

Tell me, where do you come from?

Sandile Memela

Something in me is unmistakably township; Soweto to be precise. This identity, this belonging, often finds me at unpredictable and inconvenient moments. It is like a bullet in the back. Quick and sudden. I am never prepared. You see, there is no preparation for the way they are going to take your car or you. It is something that is always lurking out there, or lingering somewhere deep inside, haunting your soul. This Sowetoness is the voice of a part of myself that I take with me everywhere I go. It refuses to stay behind. I have tried to move on, tried to rebuild my life with new pieces. In fact, I have tried to trade vital pieces of my Soweto by relocating, moving to the suburbs for promises of safety, peace of mind and stability.

There have been many occasions when I have taken time to sit, consider and disconnect from my burdensome past. But a part of my soul is always anxious and insists that you can never leave your past behind, especially the place of your growth and development. In my new home in the suburbs, I have tried to move on, become a new person. I have tried to deal with the responsibility of raising my children, getting intimately acquainted with my rainbow nation neighbours, focusing on my individual goals to contribute to the common good, go to the gym to shed some weight, keep in touch with friends and relatives all over the country.

But there are crazy moments when I am lolling on the grass, after jogging in peaceful streets, speaking English to a white neighbour's children, getting into the Madiba Magic groove, and I am surprised by an insistent wave of identity. It sweeps over me. It is an unmistakable voice. It makes my heart skip a beat, my breath comes out in short gasps. 'I am Soweto ... I am a Sowetan.' I will always be part of that African community. I do not understand it. I cannot run away. I have thought deep and hard about it. This voice comes to me and takes over my mind. It talks of my heritage, identity, belonging and I always open my hungry soul and just embrace it. You cannot run away from who you are.

This Sowetoness seduces me with its exhortation that 'you can take them out of the townships, but you cannot take the townships out of them'. If you do not know where you come from, you cannot know where you are going. It whispers and screams at the same time, of a deep connection with the place that made me what I am.

Sitting with Nomali, an urbanised Xhosa woman who is my mother, at her kitchen on a Sunday afternoon, drinking whisky, I ask her: 'Don't you want to leave this hellhole?'

Nomali puts down the cocktail glass, freeing her callused right hand. She wipes the taste on her lips with the back of that hand and a wry smile appears. She is a strong woman, neither big nor small. She is full of too much energy for an 80-year-old. There are so few lines on her, you can't believe she is barely younger than Nelson Mandela.

157

'I am home here, in Soweto,' she replies with quiet confidence. 'Though you have moved to a better life in the suburbs, this is my home. Yes, this is my home.' Her husband, Mbokodo, who is my father, lived in this house from 1961 when the gunfire of the Sharpeville massacre was fading, though it was very fresh in his young mind. He died in 1995 from heart failure after voting Nelson Mandela into the presidency. The way she talks about these politics makes my heart ache. I can see from the way she reaches to pick up her whisky glass that it is true: Soweto is home, to millions.

I know that last night, wrapped in a black night in the comfort of my suburban home, as I slipped into pyjamas, and felt the hug of my little girls before they went to sleep, their black skins brushing against mine, their Zulu spiced with English words, the strong township vibe was tugging at the chords of my soul. It does not matter where you are, Soweto will always be home. At least, to us who know June 16th. The distance, the separation of years, previously whites-only suburbia, social engineering, or even transformation, cannot cut the umbilical cord.

Silently, she watches my face as my fingers reach out for the glass between us. It is not often that I share a drink with my mother. I long for this depth of conviction, for a soulful intimacy, this level of commitment to an abandoned place, a place created to destroy your sense of self, to undermine your humanity. It is a long way from 1904.

I have to learn to know how to live, even when treated as a pariah in the townships and the suburbs. When we meet, I don't want you to make a big deal of what you consider the right address. I want you to know that when that oak door swings open in the suburbs, it only leads to a semi-hotel accommodation that is yet to develop roots for my soul. I want you to know that I have the courage, the desire to be known as a township product made good, especially from Soweto. You have to know because many want to deny where they come from, and want to distance themselves from the matchboxes of their dreams.

Well, this realisation comes from the depth of my soul, I do not understand why you have to be surprised. All my life, I have sat in that kitchen, with or without my mother, waiting for the identity, the consciousness to mature. It has come, at last, and will always be with me. It helps to know where you come from. There will be no moments when you do not know where you are going. I am not afraid to tell you that the right path to reach my soul is through Soweto. All the journey, the struggle towards a better future for all, is via Soweto. I cannot leave the place behind because it will never abandon me. Though kill me, it may.

More than a decade has passed since I stood in the heart of a newspaper office with an accusatory finger pointing at those with suitcases packed, drooling good-naturedly, propped up by their newfound riches and status, ready to fly out of what they condemned as an apartheid-created ghetto. 'We did not choose to be,' they said. They were defying the old Group Areas Act.

But I had no grand plan beyond reminding everyone that we cannot achieve success until we have laid proper foundations by redecorating the poverty of the matchboxes and garages that made us. I was a man suspended, unable to decide whether it was a right to love and leave Soweto. I had hoped that most of its lucky children would leave the darkness only when there was enough light to show the glow of a 'better life for all'.

At high-profile functions I glanced at those who had turned their backs and all they could hear from me was, 'You betrayed the future by leaving.' My voice was big and resounding with presumptuous political correctness. 'You want us to stay on so that we could be murdered by our own brothers,' they sneered. 'You want only whites to enjoy the fruits of freedom. We have a right to live where we want. After all, this is our country.' Their words were cruel, and they drained me. We were at a crossroads; I did not know which way to go.

'I am not saying don't leave Soweto. I just know that you cannot go without having laid a good, solid foundation for those who are staying behind,' I argued. I wanted to say that the path to a better life for all lies through Soweto. I was withering inside myself; I wanted those lucky devils to do more for their own community.

I felt like a lone voice crying in the wilderness. The growing light of change and transformation shone on the comfort of blackness and self-consciousness. Even Nelson Mandela left. All of a sudden, after more than three centuries, it was a rainbow nation. I waited for the familiar conscientisation to keep them awake at night, to make them return to Soweto.

But when they did not return, I picked up my suitcases too, and walked away from the poverty, hunger, hopelessness, rape, murder, after-tears parties, hijackings, funerals and unveilings.

It was a slow, painful decision. It was a move that they have always raised with me. After almost ten years, I finally left towards the end of the nineties. They were shocked. I was mocked. I gave them a blank stare and reminded them that Soweto is not a geographical location. Instead, it is a reflection of a mental attitude and a lifestyle. Yes, it is part of the soul, something that will be with you even if you did not pack it into your suitcase. They looked at me as if I was making this up, trying to intellectualise bullshit.

So I redefined my leaving. In my travels, sojourns around the globe, I have become a child of the townships. Tell me, where do you come from? When I reach out to introduce myself I say: 'I am Soweto ... I am from Soweto.' I am not afraid to open the door wide to who I am, where I come from. From the beginning, I have to tell each man I meet what to expect. 'I am Soweto.' Don't judge me by the bad things that happen there. But know that I find peace by leaving, and by knowing that I can return to the place that makes me tick.

Sandile Memela worked for the *Sowetan*, *Sunday World* and *City Press* over the past fifteen years. A graduate of Fort Hare and Stellenbosch Universities, he won fellowships to the United States and the United Kingdom. He is married to Bonnie, has four children and lives in Midrand.

How I hate the place

Eric Miyeni

I was born in Soweto and if there is such a thing as a psychological genetic code, my Soweto upbringing would be it. But it is so difficult for me to write about my childhood township.

I grew up in an asbestos-roofed, three-roomed house in Soweto. Most weekends involved watching drunken death stabbings of neighbours over girlfriends and old grudges of no real importance. Monday trips to school often meant walking past weekend corpses that had not yet been claimed by relatives or collected by the authorities. In addition, I had to duck and dive from glue-sniffing young hooligans who wanted to rob me of my meagre food money and tear my books apart.

If I lost my shoes at the beginning of the month, in the middle of winter, I was going to have to hop skip and jump my way to school for more than twenty days over icy dew, barefoot because my parents could not do much about it until the end of the month. I was lucky. Many of my schoolmates would be freezing barefoot right through the winter.

Why do I find it difficult to write about Soweto?

The place makes me feel ashamed. It's one of the true symbols of racist triumph over innocent victims. Yes, we danced. We even had the odd birthday party and, come Christmas, we got new clothes and ate well. We even had highly educated people and very rich businessmen in our midst. Soweto, as most people will tell you, was full of life. But for me, most of this vitality was a desperate attempt to survive an unwarranted hostility from a sick and sickening enemy.

If I could wave a magic wand and make a wish come true, it would be to wipe Soweto off the face of the earth and have leafy suburbs for all its residents. I hate the place with an unfathomable passion because it reminds me of my oppressor's hold over me as I wriggled in pain under his grinning red face.

Eric Miyeni lives and works in Johannesburg. He is the publishing editor of the online ezine O'*mandingo*!

Coming from the country

Phangisile Mtshali

Most people know me as a Zulu girl, who just works in Johannesburg but has roots in the Midlands of KwaZulu-Natal. Truth is, my connection with Soweto dates back to when I was still a sparkle in my parents' eyes.

You see, my mother was born in Emasakeni in 1942 where Rockville now stands. She grew up at the nearby Mofolo Village. My father hailed from the rural areas deep in KwaZulu-Natal's Midlands, eMnambithi. He came to Johannesburg to work, just like I did decades later, in 1987.

I cannot recall my first encounter with Soweto. I've been told that my mother left Soweto when she was eight months pregnant with me, to make her new home at her in-laws' home in Roosboom.

My earliest memories are not of the bustling township, but of the excitement as we prepared for the journey. I remember us catching the fattest chicken in the coop and my mother kneading the dough for a fluffy dumpling for our provisions. I was singing at the top of my voice, anticipating the trip to Johannesburg. I remember *S'cathamiya* music competing with *mbaqanga* and traditional seSotho songs on *magida s'bhekane* (third class coaches reserved for us blacks). I was going to see my father, maternal grandparents, aunts, my half-sister Nunu, cousin Vusi and other cousins but it was not the destination that excited me, but the journey.

When we arrived in Mofolo Village, around Crossroads, I was hit by claustrophobia. The houses were too close together: my mother's three-roomed home attached to another; another family's door barely a few metres away. There was loud music, the shops bustled and the staple food seemed to be *atchaar*, pickled mango and *amagwinya*, fat cakes.

The Soweto sky seemed to hang so close to the rooftops and was not the clear blue I knew back home. To my toddler eyes dark clouds hovered above us as we woke up. They would dissipate into streaks of light grey during the day. And at the time that I would have experienced a tranquil sunset back home, they would return to smother us. This was the time when streams of well-dressed people would materialise and the dirt streets would seem to come to life.

I could not understand it. In Roosboom early morning was the time the village came to life, with women and men herding cattle, flocking to the fields with hoes, sickles and water cans. At sunset we were all in our yards, munching on our harvest or watering our gardens. But in Soweto, the dark sky brought the place to life.

Vusi, who was about a year older than me, was one of the most knowledgeable children I knew. He could recite in English and he also disappeared with the morning sky and returned with the afternoon one to proudly announce: 'At crèche today we did this and that . . .' He would show me the games he played at crèche, like spinning top. He could even sing in that strange language called English.

165

My grandfather, Klaas Mthethwa, was always immaculate in his Florsheim shoes and Sunday best. He also spoke English and was widely known as Black Mamba.

Looking at the two, one young and the other old, I would start worrying that perhaps I was losing out by not living in Soweto – a short-lived regret as the sky would always come so close to the house that I would long for the clear blue skies and clean air of Roosboom.

There were women with mealies on big enamel dishes shouting 'Mbona Mkhos!' Very strange because back home maize mealies came straight from my family's fields, behind the house, or from the fields along the river or below the mountains of *Gudlintaba*. What kind of mealies were they that came from dishes on women's heads?

The fuel also puzzled me. Back home we walked long distances to fetch wood from a forest and, now and then in winter, a truck would come with sacks of coal. Here coal was sold by the shovel from rickety carts drawn by scrawny horses. Boys on the carts would be shouting at the tops of their voices 'Malaaahle!'

I couldn't get the incessant sounds of Soweto out of my head: the hooting cars, the grinding trains, shouts of drunks, loud music, hearty laughter, *Mbona Mkhozi!* and *Malaaaaahle!*

Of course, there are later memories; for example, when I was a flower girl at the wedding of one of my older cousins. There was live music, beautiful clothes, *ting* – sour porridge – and stew. It was very different from the weddings back home, where there was a cappella singing and lead vocalists would prance in front wielding sjamboks.

I also visited Soweto when I was about eight years old. My grandfather would send Nunu to the bottle store for a half jack of Oudemeester brandy – *Indoda yempandla*. My sister and I could not enter the bottle store as we were under age. So we spent what seemed like hours asking people going into the bottle store to buy us the half jack. One gentleman took pity on us and bought it, but as he was giving the bottle to Nunu it fell and shattered on the ground. We waited for hours for grandma to return from work and give us money to replace the booze. She had enough money for only a nip and I knew we were going to get a hiding.

Then there was 1976. As Soweto was going up in flames we were uprooted from Roosboom under the Group Areas Act to a shanty town called eZakheni. The battles in Soweto struck a chord in me. I could understand the anger they felt, I identified with Soweto and started seeing them as another part of my community, which was a few years ahead of us.

Ten years later, in 1986, I visited Soweto to bury my cousin Vusi, who was killed at the age of nineteen in the upheavals, *izibhelu*. I marvelled as I saw teenagers take over the funeral and dictate to our elders where, when and how Vusi was going to be buried. I returned home to Ladysmith convinced that life in Soweto and elsewhere would never be the same again. Young people in Soweto were no longer children revelling in the joys of growing up but they had assumed roles they were barely ready to take. They had power and authority way beyond their years. They were accustomed to death and they took it as a natural part of their lives.

A year later I got very close to Soweto as I joined the *Sowetan* as a women's page reporter. I got to know that the clouds that hung over it were from pollution from coal stoves.

I frequented Funda Centre, the Careers Centre and Ipelegeng Community Centre. I met people dedicated to improving their communities. I wept as I recorded vicious internecine battles. But I smiled as Soweto emerged in the mid-nineties as the epitome of the resilience of the black spirit.

Phangisile Mtshali studied journalism and worked for print and electronic media for seven years. She moved to corporate public relations and is now the Director of Bristol-Myers Squibb Foundation for a regional HIV/AIDS philanthropic programme, Secure the Future.

167

Speakiteasy days

Peter Nkomo

It is January 5, 1976 and South Africa is introducing an amazing, miraculous talking box to its citizens, after an eight month test stint. Some late Afrikaner leaders must be turning in their graves after predicting, correctly, that the devil monster called television would only be allowed in South Africa over their dead bodies.

Oh yes, I remember very well when Bophuthatswana television came on air a few years later, in 1984. I was living in Zola township; we used to call it 'United States of Zola' as it was quite a huge part of Soweto. And very famous too, with musicians like Margaret Singana, no-name jazzbands and house bands which used to play at parties, weddings and *stokvels*. There were gangsters and territories by the names of 'Sodom and Gomorrah' and 'Mshayazafe', meaning 'beat him till he's dead'.

We did not own a television set but our neighbour was

one of those fortunate few who did. But his television was beginning to give him problems, producing blurred pictures, moving itself out of frequency and so on. A friend was a real jack of all trades for radio repairs, house fumigation, playing the trumpet and bass guitar brilliantly (and he was an excellent boozer from dawn till the sun goes to bed) came up with a suggestion.

He owned an air compressor and an air blower. As he was unscrewing the back of the television box to blow the dust off, the owner was behind him. This was the first time he had seen the box stripped naked. He was anxiously waiting to be the first to witness these people who stay in this small box, who start to talk when it is 'plugged on'.

I looked at him with concern, trying to figure out his wild imagination. He belongs to the generation who first heard such ghosts when the first radios were introduced in the township communities, when they broadcast only one hour per day in an African language, early in the morning.

Looking back on life in Soweto in those speakeasy days, it brings back memories and stories. Whenever one of our friends' elders went on holiday we would gather together in his house pretending to be guarding it. We would play all sorts of games and booze all day long. We would take turns to make something to fill up our bellies at the end of the day.

But one day we ended up in beds, on couches and on mats on the floor, all with empty bellies, yes empty bellies! All because our cook that day, failed to distinguish the difference between two liquids when cooking our eggs. Oil and vinegar looked the same to the cook, who really respected only a third liquid, in the brandy bottle on the table next to him. His vision became blurred, his sense of smell was confused, and we got eggs fried in vinegar.

But he was not the only one to oil it up. The Johannesburg municipality of Soweto was graced with two types of watering holes, like most other townships. One was called a bar and

169

sold African beer, brewed by the Johannesburg municipality. Each beer carton was stuffed with a pill for longer shelf life, though some people said that the pill was made to make drinkers impotent.

The other one was called a beer lounge. Here strict rules of civilisation were enforced, like hanging a rope of honour around your neck. A tie was the dress code. The Soweto municipal police we called 'the Black Jacks' because of their black uniform, big and shining black boots and black jackets with copper buttons. They stood at the gate and made sure you had a tie on when you entered. Welcome to the civilised beer world!

One of these Soweto wells was famous. The Dube Beer Lounge was well placed next to the Dube railway station. It made it easy coming back from work, and you felt obliged to go 'register' there before proceeding home. It took up a corner of the infamous Dube hostel, a stone's throw from the Oppenheimer Gold Miners' official quarters. Those officials began their afternoon at the beer lounge, then went to their sleeping and resting quarters.

What made this place a focal point were the musical groups which entertained the patrons, groups like Harare, In-Laws, The Beaters and many more. Don't forget the pub meal, in case by the time you arrived home the family was fast asleep.

But enforced civilisation was not what it seemed. In such a lounge only a third of a capacity crowd would be wearing ties. We had a trick to pass the Black Jacks at the door. One man went in, wearing his tie, then collected a dozen more from drinkers inside. Once you were in, the rope of honour was no longer a deal. Then he took the ties back out, to a dozen men waiting to come in. Such a courier could grease 50 to 80 cents for his services, and the process would go on all evening. What was this enforced civilisation, pretending some people are more civilised than others? It reminds me of a writer who told of some animals more equal than others. Speakiteasy!

Peter Nkomo has lived in different townships within Soweto. He worked as a photographer for *City Press* and *Drum* magazine, and later for internationals like the *Sunday Telegraph* and the *Chicago Tribune*. He presently works for the Johannesburg bureaus of the *Chicago Tribune* and the *Daily Telegraph*.

Weekend traffic

Mfanasibili Nkosi

It's common nowadays to be stuck in traffic jams, particularly over the weekends in Soweto. I've always wondered where all those vehicles come from, considering the majority of Sowetans do not have jobs, and those that did have lost them in the competitive emerging economy of latter-day South Africa. I've lived here almost all my life, and I know for a fact that Sowetans have been largely dependent on the unregulated minibus taxi industry. Alas!

On a typical Saturday morning it's no surprise to be stuck for hours on one of the very few main roads in Soweto, Old Potchefstroom, waiting for long funeral processions to pass by. It is our culture to treat the dead with the utmost respect and courtesy on their final journey. Finally you get a chance, you think, to move on with your life. But, as sure as night follows day, yet another convoy led by the one we all dread to be in, a hearse – though it's our only way out of here if we're lucky – comes driving past. The other road users, myself included, try to be ever-patient.

Soweto is a by-product of the Group Areas Act, one of the harshest laws introduced by the apartheid government, to regulate where people could live based on the colour of their skin. Large numbers of black people were forcibly removed from Sophiatown, once it was declared an exclusive white area, to the makeshift townships now known as Soweto. As a result its development surprised everyone and, since then, everything about it has been playing catch-up.

As I wait in my car for the funeral cortège to go by, I daydream and start my musings. There are only three cemeteries in Soweto, Avalon being the largest and the most commonly used. It's estimated that these cemeteries serve around three and a half million people, although officially that figure is one and a half million. There aren't enough main arteries: Old Potch is the only road to access Avalon. It's the same story with the other two cemeteries. With death wreaking havoc – attributed by some to a big 'new' disease with a little name and by others to the murderous, violent culture of people of my ilk – we are fast running out of burial space. This has even led the well-heeled to bury their loved ones in cemeteries formerly reserved for whites only. West Park is the preferred one, located about twenty-five kilometres north-east of Soweto. But I suspect space is not the only culprit; status may well be another reason, because white in South Africa is still generally associated with affluence.

When news of a death reaches a relative, a friend, a neighbour and the community, it is common culture and tradition to offer condolences to the family of the deceased. It is collective moral responsibility, coined *ubuntu*, that compels people to show support for the bereaved family. This normally takes a number of days, culminating on the actual day of burial, usually over the weekend. This practice is a noble one. It is as old as our ancient rural villages, where people used to

173

walk to the graveyard en masse. But cosmopolitan Soweto changes that picture somewhat, to the detriment of an otherwise peaceful, sad and dignified funeral procession. The advent of motor cars, the constant battle for living space, competition for resources, rushing for groceries, an emergency and all the other social pressures that lead people to use the road, come to mind as I sit in the weekend traffic jam, my car idling.

Still deep in thought, I'm distracted by a taxi driver whose *ubuntu* has gone out the window. He squeezes past the intersection just as the next long, very long, convoy of mourners – right-of-way still guaranteed of course – approaches. One can tell by the brand, type, age and number of vehicles in any such procession whether the deceased was well known or not. This leads my eyes to the car adjacent to mine. The driver, who has also been stuck on one of the small streets intersecting with Old Potch Road, looks at me as if to say 'please don't let this funeral cortège be of a once-popular person.' I tell myself 'this is surely not sustainable. Imagine if I had to rush to . . .' but I don't. So I switch off the engine and let those lying still go by. But I think: I must meet the town planner one day.

Mfanasibili Nkosi is a producer for ZDF German Television, in Johannesburg. He was born, third child, and raised in Soweto. Shortly after finishing school he worked for Visnews, now Reuters television news agency. He is married, with a baby boy, and lives in one of Johannesburg's northern suburbs.

Kgosietsile's haircut

Milton Nkosi

Kgosietsile is my son. His name means 'the King has come'. He was born in a private clinic in the northern suburbs of Johannesburg in February 2001. Thirty-five years previously, in the same month, I was born in house number 9982b Ntombela Street, Orlando West, Soweto. The neighbourhood was known as Mzimhlophe. Kgosi was born in the year when passenger planes were flown into the twin towers in New York. In the year that I was born, Botswana and Lesotho won independence from British colonial rule, Nelson Mandela was spending his second year in jail and the architect of grand apartheid, Hendrik Verwoerd, was stabbed to death.

Chief, as we call Kgosi nowadays, doesn't know anything about these events and indeed nothing about South Africa's apartheid history. So I'm keen not only to teach him, but for him to experience history first-hand. I regularly take him to Soweto for his haircut. It is a huge effort because we live twenty-nine kilometres away from 1st Hair Salon on Vundla Drive, Rockville. But I want my son to know Soweto, to know where we come from and what happened there. It's immensely worrying for me to think that I may be bringing up a small black middle-class boy, who has no direct connection with his history as a black person in South Africa. You see, Chief lives in Fairlands, a comfortable suburb in north-western Johannesburg. He has his own bedroom, he has the use of a swimming pool and goes to a private crèche and speaks English. Though I'm proud to say without an accent – yet!

Soweto is critical when it comes to educating my son in the languages of his country. The place helps me to teach him Zulu, Sotho, Tswana, Swazi, Afrikaans and Tsotsitaal. All these languages are eloquently spoken in the township, because Soweto is a mixed masala, a true reflection of the composition of modern day South African society. As well as the three million black people residing there, you'll find a few white faces of priests, doctors, artists and lots of international tourists. For this reason I love Soweto: it's where my son can get his bearings.

There are many black middle-class people in the new South Africa who regard living in the suburbs, away from the townships, as a form of status. It separates them from the ugly apartheid past. They enjoy listening to their children speak English with an English accent, or a kugel accent – that spoken by white women from Sandton and the surrounding boom-fenced suburbs. Well, we differ. Mkotjo Mota, one of my closest friends also takes his sons Mota and Lebo to Soweto for their haircuts. We form part of a group of South Africans who want their families to be very much connected to their past. As Bob Marley once sang: *In this great future we can't forget our past.* It is the country of my soul.

Our route to Rockville takes us on the N1 South highway and we exit at the Nasrec off-ramp and drive through Diepkloof extension, the poshest area in the township. Many people in

Soweto aspire to own a house there. Then we go to the old Diepkloof, Zone 5. Here houses have three rooms of inferior dark grey brick, unplastered since they were built by the government in the early fifties. On past Baragwanath taxi rank onto Old Potch Road. The rank is full of hundreds of minibus taxis. Chief sees for himself how many black people live here. He sees one of the biggest hospitals in the world, Chris Hani Baragwanath, where his mother works as a paediatrician in the children's ward. The nurses' building alone is twelve storeys high. Now Chief can see the township herdsman looking after his animals. Goats crossing the tarred road, with the latest car models winding through them.

We reach Orlando garage, famous for its incredibly tasty fish and chips! Sometimes we buy *spy-kos* (fast food in tsotsitaal) for the guys at the salon. Chief can see the shining roofs of Motsoaledi squatter camp, named after ANC veteran Elias Motsoaledi who was from Orlando West. There are no running water or sewerage facilities there. Women walk with yellow 20-litre drums of water on their heads. It seems easy but it's an amazing skill to carry that and walk upright with both hands free to take care of other chores. Those women have a special balancing act to do on a daily basis. They used to fetch cooking water from the local stream, sharing it with dogs, donkeys and goats; now at least they have a stand pipe and clean running water.

Old Potch road cuts through Soweto from Diepkloof, Orlando East, Pimville, Klipspruit, Dlamini, Chiawelo and reaches out to Protea. It used to be the only passage to the North West province and it runs to an end in the small university town of Potchefstroom, FW de Klerk's university. I doubt he ever contemplated visiting our township in his student days.

Chief casts his eyes to the right and he sees an old power station, Orlando Power Park. It is smack in the middle of Soweto, but it used to feed electrical power to white Johannesburg. Black residents in Soweto would pay more than double

177

the price for power because it had to be drawn from a distant grid. Sowetans were treated as second class citizens because they were black. Orlando Power Station had a huge dam but black people were by law not allowed to fish from the dam. White people could. They drove from the suburbs to have the best catch of the day, while surrounded by a township population larger than that of Namibia's.

Now we see Vista, the only university in the township. It's a government institution and many black students owe their success to it. Next door is the Soweto Teachers' Training College. People studied against all odds, even when they were fed 'Bantu Education', an inferior standard designed by Hendrik Verwoed to kill the brain of a black man. He failed, of course.

Chief sees Bethesda Children's Home, where the Salvation Army looks after AIDS orphans. One result of stigma around HIV/AIDS in the townships is that young mothers dump their newborns in dustbins or with strangers. Few want to raise an HIV-positive baby whose life is going to be short, probably under two years without antiretroviral treatment. Bethesda home is a small oasis. Major Theresa Jwili, who runs the orphanage, once told me she worked there even though she was surrounded by so much pain and despair, 'because I'm a mother and a grandmother myself, and also to offer hope because without it there's nothing to live for.' She and her staff are a pillar of strength in an otherwise extremely depressing environment.

Now we approach the notorious Killer Road Intersection officially known as Klip Valley Road. This is the main artery from Dlamini, Klipspruit and other townships to Orlando West and Noordgesig. It has seen too many accidents. In the early eighties motorists, especially minibus taxi drivers, used the road long before it was officially opened and earned it the Killer nickname.

Chief can see a church with newly renovated pitch black roof tiles. This is Regina Mundi, home to many anti-apartheid meetings. I remember Archbishop Desmond Tutu addressing me and hundreds of others in the mid-eighties. I tell Chief about its history; he doesn't understand but he can feel the passion. We are nearly there. We pass Moroka police station, where I was once an inmate after taking part in a student protest, and soon turn into Vundla Drive. There is Elkah Stadium, the only cricket oval in Soweto. Sadly South Africa's team is still very white in terms of players. I'm yet to see black kids from the townships coming through the ranks, so cricket is still a two nations sport. When the English team once came to play in Soweto, they had more black players than the South African team. That's unacceptable.

Finally we arrive at 1st Hair Salon. Iggy Khoali, the owner, is at the door and he shouts 'Heita Chief!' A tiny voice shouts from the back seat of the car 'Heita Iggy!' I feel fulfilled to hear my son greet in the language that I used when I was young. Pat and Mike Lekoto are brothers and they both work with Iggy at the salon. They are keen to get Chief to speak more township lingo beyond just heita. They tease him about where he comes from and when he tries a few words there's laughter. He gets his haircut, a number one style on the clipper. I get mine and we are complete. Chief walks out and says 'Sharp, sharp, Iggy!' with a thumbs up sign.

When we leave Rockville we drive through Mofolo to Orlando West to see if we can get a bit of lunch at my mother's house. Bridgette Motshegoa Nkosi lives with my beloved sister Senele and they run a small textile store in downtown Jo'burg. The debate in the family is what happens when we win the Lotto. Senele says she stays in Soweto. My mother loves the township but wants to follow her three sons into the suburbs while she keeps her house in the township. My brothers and I chickened out of the township but we spend a lot of our time there for weddings, funerals and family gatherings. So we say we sleep in the suburbs, but we live in Soweto. The debate continues!

Milton Nkosi is the BBC's Bureaux Chief in Africa. He was educated in South Africa and did part of his journalism and management training in London. He studied teaching and civil engineering before he joined the BBC. Milton has covered many wars around the continent and beyond including the 2003 war in Iraq. He is married and has two children. He lives in Johannesburg.

But I live in Soweto

Elizabeth Ohene

It took me a while to get to Soweto. But then it took quite a while to get to South Africa, when I stop to think about it. The BBC African Service first applied for a visa for me to visit South Africa on a duty tour in 1987. But it wasn't the most opportune time for journalists to be asking for reporting visas. And I was travelling on a Ghanaian passport which had imprinted boldly on its pages: 'Not valid for travel to the Republic of South Africa or the Bantustans'. But thanks to the intervention of Helen Suzman, I was granted a visa in October 1989 and arrived on the first of what was to become many reporting trips.

Of course I wanted to go to Soweto, the Soweto about which I had made so many telephone calls to people in the pursuit of news stories. I was desperate to see and feel the real thing. After a week in a hotel in town my friends the Mazwais, whom I had first met over the phone, took me to their home in Soweto. I lived there and commuted into town daily. After a few days, I was feeling quite proud. I could drive by myself to Soweto without getting lost, I knew all the landmarks and I instinctively removed my seat belt so it wouldn't be obvious that I wasn't a local.

That is how it came about that I was driving my hired car on a Friday evening, at about eleven, from town to my new home. Soon after going off the expressway I met a long queue of vehicles. It was one of those notorious police roadblocks that were so common at entrances to townships at that time, a legacy of the state of emergency.

A policeman walks up, peers into the car and asks me where I'm going.

'Home, officer.'

'Your ID?'

I hesitate and explain that I don't have one.

'Is that meant to be a joke? Your ID!'

'Er . . . I'm not South African, and my passport isn't with me this minute.'

Now the policeman is incredulous.

'Yes, I am going home. I am visiting from London and I am staying with my friends in Soweto.'

'How can you be visiting from London and staying in Soweto? What exactly are you doing here?'

I fumbled for a couple of minutes and tried not to disclose my identity. I was anxious not to admit to being a journalist, but eventually gave way.

'I am a BBC reporter and I am in your beautiful country on duty. I am staying with my friends in Soweto. Here is my BBC ID.'

A few more policemen cluster round.

'But you can't stay in Soweto.'

'Why can't I?'

'Strangers don't stay in Soweto. It is not possible to be visiting South Africa and staying in Soweto. You are supposed

182

to be in a hotel.'

I tried to explain that my friends were in Soweto, but the policeman will not conceive it is possible. A friend in Melville, Sandton or Rosebank, yes, but not That Place.

'You cannot be a BBC reporter and stay in Soweto.'

'But I do.'

'You BBC people are nothing but trouble. Supposing something happens to you now, we in South Africa will be blamed. You know Soweto is not safe and you are here so late in the night telling me you are staying in Soweto.'

'Believe me, officer, where I live in Soweto it is quite safe and all the neighbours are very friendly.'

'You cannot stay in Soweto, it is not allowed. Let's take a look in the boot of your car.'

I get out reluctantly, resigned to the prospect of spending the night by the roadside or at the police station. I open the car boot; they shone their torches inside and pick out a bundle.

'What is this?'

And so I have my idea.

'BBC T-shirts, would you like some? Here, I think the extra large ones will be suitable and you can take a small size each for a child at home.'

'Okay, okay, on your way then; but really, you are not supposed to be in Soweto.'

'But officer, I do live in Soweto.'

Three days later, six famous political prisoners are released and I am reporting from the home of Walter Sisulu. When he gets to his home after twenty-seven years of jail I am introduced to him. He asks if I had come all the way from Ghana. I am able to answer: 'No Sir, I live in Soweto.'

Elizabeth Ohene, a Ghanaian journalist, worked for the BBC African Service from 1986 to 2000, mostly in London, and was a

well-known voice on African Service programmes like *Focus on Africa* and *Network Africa*. She reported from South Africa during its transition in 1993 and 1994. She is now state minister of tertiary education in Ghana.

Three views from afar

Justin Pearce

I grew up in the southern suburbs of Cape Town, as far from Soweto as you can get, physically and spiritually, without leaving South Africa. It must have been 1976 – I was nine – when I first heard the name of the place. It was where they had riots. Then the riots came to Cape Town. Trips into town would be cancelled because 'there's trouble'. My father would come home from work red-eyed after the teargas in Darling Street was sucked up a lift-shaft and into his office. The riot police wore brown camouflage against the city's granite and asphalt. We had riot drill at school: line up behind the bookcase if 'they' start throwing things through the windows, and assemble outside in an orderly fashion if they are trying to burn the place down.

About fifteen years later I was travelling home by whatever means possible after visiting a friend in Harare. I took an early bus to Masvingo and spent the day nosing around the ruins of Great Zimbabwe. I had been assured there was a bus to Beit Bridge, the border, in the evening. I had not realised that in Zimbabwe good manners require giving a positive rather than a truthful answer to questions. There was no bus. Some Seventh-Day Adventists saw me looking lost in the summer dusk, warned me about the presence of *tsotsis* and took me home to their house in the township. Or high density suburb, as townships are called in Zimbabwe.

'Where are you from?' one of the Seventh-Day Adventists asked me.

'Cape Town,' I said.

'Is that near Soweto?' he asked hopefully. The South African township's reputation loomed large north of the Limpopo.

I was forced to disappoint him.

Ten years after that I went to work in Angola. There I got to know Boavista, a township in Luanda. Or bairro, as townships are called in Angola. There is an essential difference though. In South Africa, the government built the townships. In Angola the people built the bairros. At least that's what they did in Boavista. People had saved to buy a sack of cement this month, a piece of corrugated zinc the next; they had moulded concrete blocks, dried them in the sun, put them together with mortar oozing out between. Sometimes they painted them in the pastel colours of the Portuguese empire and decorated them with shells pressed into the cement. Then they saved for a gilt plastic clock on the wall and a washtub in the backyard.

But the Angolan government was pulling the bairros down. Men with sledgehammers came and flattened Boavista because there was money to be made from the site's great views of the Atlantic ocean and of the sunset. Luxury housing was to take its place. The people were sent to live in tents outside the city where there were no jobs. There was also no running water and no electricity, but that wasn't so different from life in the bairros. The townships of Luanda are the kind of place

186

where 20 litres of water, delivered on a truck, can cost more than a day's wages.

Electricity? In my flaking concrete middle-class flat in central Luanda the power worked half the time. That wasn't much help to the lady who came from one of the bairros to do my laundry, who didn't know what the sockets in the wall were for, or why the clothes iron had a flex and a plug attached.

Once I travelled home overland by whatever means possible, from Angola through Namibia to South Africa. As my minibus came into Windhoek, Namibia's capital, I saw light shining from Katatura township. It was clear that we were no longer in Angola as electricity was no longer the preserve of the few.

Back in South Africa, I paid a visit to Soweto, meeting activists who were campaigning against high electricity bills for residents. Under apartheid, those who had power refused to pay for it as a way of protesting against the system. Now more people were wired up, but the government was cutting supplies from those who couldn't scrape cash together to pay bills. But here I was, in a poor neighbourhood with the unfamiliar sight of electrical cables slung above boxy houses.

Old Ellen's electricity had been cut off, she said, so she was using candles and a paraffin stove on the empty floor of her home. This did look familiar, so familiar to me that I had to bite my tongue not to address her in Portuguese. Down the road, Lindiwe was home on parole from a prison sentence for petty theft; still unemployed, she now owed 13 000 rand (over 1000 American dollars) for the electricity her teenage son had used in her absence.

I was a journalist tagging along with a delegation from a foreign non-governmental organisation. We visited the Mandelas' house, the Hector Petersen memorial, the whole struggle tourism circuit. In Boavista, people had stood by, impotent, as their houses were knocked down. Here in Soweto the momentum of twenty-five years of full-time struggle had

187

spawned a small industry. People were reconnecting the electricity supplies of those who had been cut off because of unpaid bills.

Mabel still used the word struggle. 'I started joining the struggle because I can see there is no freedom in this country. I voted ANC thinking we would have changes in this country because we voted black people in. In the past we would say we were living under apartheid...now we are oppressed by our own black people we call our government.'

She asked me what Angola was like. I told her that no one in a township there could expect to have electricity.

'So that's why they all want to come here,' she said.

Justin Pearce started out as a journalist working for the now-defunct Cape Town weekly *South*, and later for the *Mail & Guardian* in Johannesburg. More recently he spent two years as the BBC correspondent in Angola. He lives in Johannesburg, and is completing a book about Angola during the transition from war to peace.

188

Township golf

Marcus Prior

There is a golf course in Soweto. 'It's not very green, not like the courses in the rest of Johannesburg, but it's playable,' says Irvin Mosate, a young professional who grew up playing golf at Soweto Country Club and dreams of competing alongside Tiger Woods. Woods turned the white game of golf and the cosy world of the country club on its head. But Soweto's 18-hole golf course was around long before Tiger tamed a sporting world that, in less enlightened times, would have had him barred.

The story of black golf in South Africa is in many ways unremarkable. The everyday pursuits of white society were mirrored in the townships. Even golf. Often the reality was little more than a dusty stretch of open land, an improvised target and a motley selection of rusty, hand-me-down clubs begged, borrowed or stolen from someone more fortunate. But the game of golf itself does not discriminate between skin colour. Anyone can get the bug.

What is remarkable is how much has been achieved with so little. At the heart of it all has been Soweto CC. For years it was the only course where black golfers could play unhindered on a daily basis, unrestricted by pass laws and prejudice. Elsewhere caddies got only limited permission to play a quick nine holes. And as white golfers played for substantial purses on their established tour, black golfers competed for a few rand, most often at Soweto CC.

'I won my first competition with a last round 68 at Soweto and never looked back from there on,' says Theo Manyama, a successful black professional and now tournament director on the fully integrated Sunshine Tour, southern Africa's professional golf circuit. 'The winner of those tournaments would win about fifteen rand and there would probably be three prizes in all, or five if the field was big.'

The lack of golf courses did not always mean a lack of golf clubs. It is a measure of the passion for the game among black South Africans that bodies were formed even if they had nowhere to play. Talking about the game was sometimes all that was possible. 'We had golf clubs but we didn't belong to any golf course,' Manyama says of his early days in Soweto. 'I lived in Diepkloof and we formed the Diepkloof Golf Club even though there was no course there. We used to choose the home of one of our wealthier members as a clubhouse and we'd go there and have some meetings, probably because we knew he could afford to make us some tea!'

Manyama is one of a generation of golfers that struggled against overwhelming odds to make a living from the game. Vincent Tshabalala was perhaps the most successful, winning the French Open in 1976, but there were many others. In the yet-to-be-built Hall of Fame of black South African golf, names such as Shadrack Molefe, Richard Moerane, Solly Sepeng and John Mashego will resonate loudly.

Much as Soweto CC was their home, to cut it as pro-

190

fessionals the best black players knew they needed experience on courses beyond the township if they were to compete properly. Invitations to 'white' tournaments came, slowly, but were often a double-edged sword. Manyama refused an invitation to play in South Africa's PGA Championship in 1970 because he knew he was not ready. 'It was so hard to go from sand greens to grass. The difference is unbelievable. We didn't even have fairways or rough, let alone water hazards.'

He was right. Four black golfers did accept invitations and Manyama watched them struggle to break one hundred. It was exactly what he had feared: embarrassing. The truth is few, if any, black golfers of Manyama's era were able to make a living from the game. They played golf because they loved the sport and were addicted to the buzz of a birdie and the fizz of a shot struck so pure it could never be bettered – until the next one. But more than all of that, Manyama and his Soweto friends knew they were blazing a trail. 'We suffered and stuck it out,' he says. 'We said to ourselves that we were paving the way for those who would come after us. We were chased out of golf courses, we'd play on Mondays when we'd be dodging sprinklers and we didn't even know driving ranges existed.'

'The truth is sometimes I still think that I'm dreaming when I see how things have turned around. I worry that I'll wake up and discover I'm not even a tournament director and that I don't work for the Tour. We didn't believe this was possible, there was not even the smallest dream of it. Today, I am happy. I'm happy that all youngsters today need do is to work hard. The facilities are there and help is there, it's all staring them in the face. We can have a Tiger Woods from the black players in South Africa.'

Bafana Hlophe is one of those youngsters, a modern professional who is still proud to claim Soweto CC as his home, the course where he learned the game which is now his life. 'Soweto Country Club is my lovely place, I am so

191

proud of it,' he says. 'I practise there, spend most of my time there and am proud to represent the club as a professional.' Like so many before him, Hlophe was a caddy first, then a golfer. If the next generation is to bypass the bag-carrying stage, Hlophe says there is still a huge divide to bridge.

'There are so many youngsters at the club but they all need help. The development board and sponsors are doing their best but there's so much needed. Kids need to realise what it takes to succeed in this game too – how much you need to practise and the time you have to spend in the gym. I thought it was easy, but now I know how hard it is.'

Ask Theo Manyama and his friends just how hard.

Marcus Prior is a writer and broadcaster who has covered sport in southern Africa for the past six years, the last four of them with the MWP Media news agency. Before that he was a producer and presenter with the BBC World Service in London and Johannesburg. At the time of writing he was in the process of leaving sport behind and packing his cases for Kenya and a job with the World Food Programme.

Jumping for joy

Ofeibea Quist-Arcton

'Whoa, steady, my dearest. Steady now. Uh-uh, you're naughty. Steady, Lady. You really have to be firm till you get them calm.' Then he whistles, almost purring, lovingly. He is Enos Mafokate, ringmaster, showjumper extraordinaire and founder of the Soweto Equestrian Academy. He is talking simultaneously to Lady, the Academy's chestnut mare, and to Zanele, a rather nervous first-time rider who says she would rather climb on horseback than play with her dolls.

That is music to the ears of Mafokate, who has earned the nicknames 'Soweto Uncle' and the 'Horserider President'. He has been passionate about horses since he was a child, when he started riding on a donkey. 'I think this thing is in my blood. I became a groom, cleaning up the muck and then I became a stable manager. I struggled.' Mafokate also works at the local branch of the Society for the Prevention of Cruelty to Animals in Soweto.

He wants to see black children in Soweto and other townships having the same opportunities as their white counterparts; opportunities that he, a talented showjumper, was denied under apartheid, because of the colour of his skin. Mafokate had his day at the Five Roses Bowl in Soweto, where some of his dreams became reality when he organised the first showjumping competition in the township, rather grandly called the Soweto Equestrian Family Day.

In 1980, Mafokate broke through the colour barrier and became the first black rider to represent South Africa in international showjumping competitions. He is proud of that and also of his trophies. But Mafokate's real triumph is the creation of the Soweto Equestrian Academy, another grand title, this time for the first horse-riding school in a township. Here the children share hats, jodhpurs, boots, laughs, Enos and, of course, the few horses that make up the stables.

The Soweto gala is a far cry from the horse and carts one can still hear clip-clopping from a distance in the township, as 'rag and bone' men collect scrap metal and just about anything else worth recycling, for a small fee. Resources are limited and sponsorship has been a problem, but there's a buzz in the air. The young black riders are excited about this first-time event in Soweto. As one mother puts it: 'We don't have much money here and we don't have enough equipment for the children. But we do have a lot of enthusiasm. The children enjoy being here.'

The Academy's prize jumper, and the most experienced horseman after Mafokate, is Phehello 'Pepe' Mofokeng. He is fourteen years old and became firm friends with Mafokate as soon as they met, brought together by their shared passion for horses. 'I really loved horses very much, but I didn't know where to go for riding lessons. I saw Enos walking around with the horse, so I followed him until he stopped and asked me why I was looking at him. When I told him I loved horses, he said I could come and run along with him. So I went, and here I am,' says Pepe.

With borrowed jodhpurs straining across his hips, sporting an oversized riding hat and holding Lady in check, Pepe smiles a slow, happy smile. 'I love it when I fall, because when I stand up I know I will be better next time!' He says he wants to be a champion and 'to teach those coming after me. When I finish school, I want to be like our trainer Enos. I want to train other kids and give them what Enos gave me. I feel very good that he taught me and look where I am now, I am in a show! And I think I'll come first or second.'

Five Roses Bowl is a neatly mown arena with white tents and white jumps adorned with flowers, leaves and fronds. It all looks so professional. A table is covered with rows and rows of red rosettes, certificates, a giant silver plate trophy and smaller cups. It looks as if every rider, regardless of ability, will carry off a memento. The judges sit at another table, equipped with a public address system.

Motley spectators include choristers singing in joyful harmony, ululating in appreciation, dancing and cheering on the riders. Local children with broad smiles and senior citizens, some with toothless grins, have also gathered alongside a few local dignitaries.

But the guests of honour are not from Soweto – nor anywhere near. Most have never set foot in the township before. These jumpers are all white, their parents and supporters from outside. Bringing the out-of-towners together with township children was one of Mafokate's dreams and he is delighted to see it happen. A few years earlier, that would have been unimaginable in Soweto. 'Honestly, this is one of the biggest things in my heart. I feel like crying, I feel like laughing. Something like this is a part of history. You see, I have got all people coming here today. I feel proud to take whites from where they are and put them together with black people,' says Mafokate.

With a shout, he gathers together his young riders and

literally takes them through the jumps. Heading the pack, animated, sweating and clutching a mobile telephone, Mafokate leaps over the white jumps, barking orders and instructions to his charges who struggle to keep up with this energetic and driven horse rider. 'Remember, right-hand side is red, left-hand side is white. Okay? Right? Thank you.'

At the other end of the grounds the white trainer is putting her riders through their paces over the jumps, unassisted. Zandra Mitchell, one of the visitors, is a natural, bareback rider with an obvious affinity for horses. At thirteen years old she is a year younger than Pepe and is in Soweto for the first time. Zandra is trying to calm a frisky horse, Panda. But she'll be jumping on Darling Buds of May, one of sixteen horses and two foals her family owns. 'Stop it, stop it now. She is a good jumper and very naughty,' Zandra says of her mount, patting her gently. In between reprimands, she shares her first impressions of Soweto. 'Oh, it's quite cool. I like the ground. It's quite nice here. Some of the horses are very nice and very well taken care of.'

The black and white riders do not mix much, but Mafokate says that will take time and it is a start. He admits he is a little disappointed with the small turnout of white people. 'It is nearly there, not exactly as big as I wanted, but something like this is part of history and more white people will start coming,' he repeats.

Would Zandra come back to Soweto? 'Well, why not?' she says, adding 'I think it's going to be very nice. I think it's going to be cool. I think it is very important for friendship, because friendship is important to other people and stuff.'

Mafokate is hopeful because he remembers the day when, as a groom, he watched only white riders showjumping, knowing in his heart that he could jump better. And he did. It took imagination and stamina, but he made it. Pepe mirrors that determination. 'I want to be a champion. I want to be a professional showjumper in South Africa and around the world.' With that he mounts the placid chestnut and trots off to compete in the 'Jump for Joy' class of Soweto's first Equestrian Family Day.

Ofeibea Quist-Arcton is from Ghana. She is the Africa correspondent of allAfrica.com and a freelance broadcaster for the BBC, with whom she has worked for twenty years. Her passions are Africa, its art, culture, literature, history, people and music. Her Johannesburg home is full of paintings, sculptures and art from all over the continent. Her dream is to be able to sing like a youthful Miriam Makeba, with all the clicks.

There goes the neighbourhood

Jon Qwelane

Once the source of dreams for many aspirant young blacks, especially males, the City of Gold has lost its lustre and has become, instead, a den of iniquity, illegal immigrants and corrupt government officials.

The Mecca where we all eventually ended up, inevitably, was Soweto. Where today the mother city of Johannesburg is bursting at the seams with illegal aliens, it was the daughter Soweto's turn yesterday to be pregnant with many 'undesirable Bantus' like me who, so the white overlords decreed, could only find happiness in the homelands.

It is interesting to note how the same reactions to parallel situations come about, and how only the names conveniently change to fit in with our prejudices: the *batswagae* or so-called home-boys which we were, was the terminology of the city slickers that fitted nicely with the apartheid masters' designs of divide-and-rule. Nowadays the same theme of 'alien Bantus' which was once ruthlessly applied to us via the pass laws, is seen in the theme of 'illegal aliens', the badge of honour of all *magrigamba* and *makwerekwere*.

The good old days are gone, and for that we have the bad new days of democracy and the 'new South Africa' to thank. Before anyone labels me with the tag of apartheid-lover and claims that I longingly miss our oppression, let me quickly say in my own self-defence that telling the truth will not make any difference, except to those who delight in shying away from it.

And the simple truth is that Jozi is not *lekker* any more. There was once a time, and it's not a hundred years ago, when there were really only two enemies one had to be on the lookout for in Soweto: a pass-demanding policeman, and a thug on the streets when you were out for a *jol* but had no extra cash.

The cop was bad news because he was intent on carting you off to chokey for a while, and out of the dazzling spells of the beautiful young student nurses at Baragwanath Hospitals' nurses' home and the ever-tempting icy cold beer of the ghetto shebeens. The thug was equally bad news because, for not having anything on you to spare for him, you risked collecting a few angry hot slaps.

But then again, the cops and thugs of the good old days were far more preferable any day to the new lot spawned by human rights and democracy. You see, in the ancient days the cops did not just shoot: they carried no guns, and depended rather on speed to nail their prey. Guns were introduced heavily only during the last decade of apartheid. The thugs had only their menacing slaps and fists and only carried a knife, which they rarely used, at least until the death of official apartheid came near.

The new human-rights and democracy-laden regime has been so lax that guns are ten a penny, and settling arguments with lead is now so common that fisticuffs as a word will soon disappear from the dictionary; as a form of physical exercise will become extinct.

We thrived on *spaai-kos* or *spy-kos* in Soweto: quick-fix grub that could be anything from fat cakes and white liver polony, to pap and offal bought at the roadside. Now, alas, you have all manner of takeaway outlets selling you *spaai-kos* all right, but because they call it 'takeaways' it is made to sound somewhat better than what we used to eat. You now have McDonald's, KFC, Chicken Licken, Pizza Hut, Wimpy, and what have you.

Of course the new human-rights environment has increased the number of 'situations' in our midst, and they are anything from president to owner of mines. In our time you had to be a teacher or clerk to qualify as a 'situation' and you owned a grocery store if you owned anything. But a mine! And if you were 'president' you headed either a debating society, or a *stokvel* group.

The good old days are gone, and we have the new South Africa and the human rights culture to thank.

Jon Qwelane is a Johannesburg journalist. He won the inaugural Nat Nakasa Award for stirring trouble. He is now with the Mogale City Council as the managing editor of *Dikgang Tsa Mogale*, a monthly community newspaper.

Passbook

Gugulakhe Radebe

'Pas! Waar is jou pas!' 'Passbook! Where is your passbook!' Cold words that sent shivers down the spine of many an African person, especially black African people.

What is this dreaded *pas*? I'll try to explain. This was the creation of apartheid South Africa to 'keep black people in their place', segregate them from other groupings. To understand this pass I will take you into South Africa of the sixties, seventies and eighties.

By law black people either belonged in a homeland or on farmlands away from the city. For one to be anywhere near the city there were some restrictions that had to be complied with. Section 10(1)A allowed the bearer of the dreaded pass to reside in the black areas around Johannesburg and Section 10(1)B allowed the bearer to be in Johannesburg but not to consider himself a resident. They were migrants. There was a sure stint in jail for whoever was asked for and could not produce the dreaded pass with the relevant stamp.

Where then does one get this pass, I hear you ask. I'll explain. The process was meant to dehumanise you through and through, literally and figuratively. I was a stocky black male and was big for my age at sixteen, so I suffered a lot at the hands of the pass-demanding South African police. As a result I had to go to the pass office a lot sooner than my peers and this is where I came face to face with the reality of the system, the apartheid system.

I am going to attempt to take you through the process. You had to get to the Albert Street Compound in downtown Johannesburg early in the morning to join the various queues of people applying for the pass. All the officials were white Afrikaners who had an IQ of two or less, but they were there because they were white.

Passport pictures were always done so that one looked as shocked as possible. To achieve this you would be asked 'what are you smiling at?' and you would frown, then 'what are you frowning at?' Then you would be slightly confused as to what they wanted you to do and that would give the perfect picture of you looking shocked and confused.

Then it was the X-ray. I really do not know how they got that thing to be so cold, but the instruction was 'hug the machine!' and obediently you would. The instruction to breathe in did not need to be bellowed out because you would breathe in anyway from the cold, thus giving the best X-ray of your lungs. If your lungs had a semblance of tuberculosis or any other infection you were sent back whence you came. If you spoke Xhosa, to Transkei. Zulu to Natal. Sotho to the Free State, called Orange Free State at the time. Shangaan to the North, even if you knew nobody there.

The next process was the worst. *'Vula-vala'* (open and close) was the instruction to those without a foreskin to show your dick to a crippled white boy who could not be more than twenty years old. He determined whether you had any sexually transmitted diseases. If so, that was also an instant ticket back to your 'homeland'.

If you made it through this process you qualified to be in Johannesburg and you could, as an adult, look for work.

My illustration of apartheid always comes from this dreaded process. I came out of *'Vula-vala'* with my clothes bunched under my arm, stark naked, and came face to face with the old man who lived opposite our house in Diepkloof. In African culture he was my 'father'; any adult male is your father, but this old man was so close to me that it almost felt like my dad was stark naked in front me. And I did not know where to hide in shame, the shame of seeing your elder naked. But this was Albert Street and we were all 'boys' there.

One could not help but shed a little tear when the brown book was issued at last, because it was in a way going to take the dreaded police off your back for a while. There would be no more weekends in police cells for me, because of the pass.

Gugulakhe Radebe is a freelance cameraman who works for ITN and the BBC, based in Johannesburg. Born in 1960 he has had the luck of going through the good and the bad days in South Africa.

A classic township

Adam Roberts

I like second-hand bookshops, especially one in Melville, tucked in beside the restaurants and cafes of that part of Johannesburg. I like to buy an old book, almost at random, then sit with a coffee in the late afternoon sun and read something unexpected. One such afternoon, about a year ago, I came across a book by a man whose subject was a squalid, crowded part of the world that I didn't know especially well. I had read it once before but was surprised to find it there.

The book, by the son of a labourer, is called *The Classic Slum* and describes life in a township a couple of years into the new century. It portrays a pretty awful place. Jammed up against a big industrial town, where jobs were hard to find, the slum itself was little more than a big dormitory for the poor. Migrants who had rushed from the countryside and from poorer countries nearby brought their own social problems and divisions.

This was a grimy city on the edge of a much more successful, affluent one. The author writes of 'the dirt that hung over all ... the rubbish that lay for months in the back alleys ... the "entries" or ginnels with open middens where starving cats and dogs roamed or died and lay for weeks unmoved'. Some houses, he goes on, 'stank so badly through an open doorway that one stepped off the pavement to pass them by. That people stayed scrupulously clean in such surroundings – and many did – only proves the tenacity of the human spirit.'

The slum was divided into different villages, some rich and leafy, others barely fit for human habitation. 'Every industrial city, of course, folds within itself a clutter of loosely defined overlapping "villages" ... streets and alleys locked along the north and south by two railway systems a furlong apart. About twice that distance to the east lay another slum which turned on its farther side into a land of bonded warehouses and the city proper.'

He quotes another writer, Friedrich Engels, who, some years before, had also written of this part of the slum: '... a mass of courts and alleys are to be found in the worst possible state'. Engels describes one man living in a cow-stable who 'had constructed a sort of chimney for his square pen, which had neither windows, floor nor ceiling, had obtained a bedstead and lived there, though the rain dripped through his rotten roof'. Those who have visited refugee camps on the edges of war, or spent some time in the worst corners of squatter camps beside big cities, like Johannesburg, might recognise that sort of description.

The place he writes about is not in Africa today, of course, but in Britain just a century ago. He describes life in Salford, a slum on the edge of the great industrial city of Manchester, in the then richest country in the world, where desperate Irish migrants crowded together during the nineteenth century with equally hungry internal migrants from the English countryside. What strikes me is how similar his description is of Salford then, to Soweto, on the edge of Johannesburg, today.

Just as Soweto is made up of several villages, the smart corners of Diepkloof extension and the rougher, more violent parts of Zola, Salford's villages also varied. Of his own corner, with a population of about 3000 people at this Edwardian time, the author of my book describes an uninspiring range of services and shops on offer. You could find fifteen shebeens (though he calls them beer houses), a hotel, two bottle stores (off-licences, as the British say), nine large spaza shops (grocery stores), a fish and chip shop, an old clothes shop and a smattering of barbers, 'tripe shops', pawnbrokers and a loan shark. As in Soweto today, funeral insurance societies were extremely important: usually women would save together against the sudden and painful cost of dealing with a death; some of these societies eventually grew to be big financial institutions. Soweto now has a few supermarkets, sports centres, laundromats, a car dealership or two, petrol stations and cellphone shops. But otherwise it does not seem so different from the township on the edge of Manchester. Engels thought it was the 'very epitome of all industrial ghettoes' and called Salford the 'Classic Slum', which is how the book I read got its title.

It was the daily life of ordinary people that most interested the author of my book, a man who describes himself as 'a dweller in that world of want when the century was new'. Salford had its fair share of troublesome people, its 'idlers, part-time beggars and petty thieves', he reflected, though it also had a strict class system which divided families according to the quality of their homes, the occupations of the adults and the education of the children. People could be prim, or pushy, or nosy; some were spiteful and delighted in the failure and mishaps of neighbours. But many were supportive, helping out when neighbours had problems.

Just as in any township, certainly those I have visited as a journalist in Africa and in Asia, including Soweto, alcohol was a big part of daily life. For Salford dwellers 'Drunkenness, rowing or fighting in the streets', was sternly disapproved of 'except perhaps at weddings and funerals (when old scores were often paid off), Christmas or bank holidays'. But drunkenness happened a great deal. Even so, the author says the 'women in the slums were far from being foul-mouthed sluts and harridans, sitting in semi-starvation at home in between trips to the pub and pawnshop' and 'nor were most men boors and drunken braggarts'.

The inhabitants of such English townships were not a healthy lot. A study in 1901 found that a quarter of the people living in York, a nearby town, lacked the 'bare necessities of life'. Another study in 1906 showed that women with jobs worked an average of fifty-five hours a week. Most children in Salford walked barefoot, many had rickets, smallpox, typhus, enteric fever, scarlet fever or diphtheria. One passage in the book, coincidentally related to South Africa, showed the ill health of the men from Manchester. In 1899 12 000 men from the city volunteered for the war the British were fighting in South Africa. Two-thirds of them were immediately rejected as obviously unfit for service. Just 1 200 were eventually found to be healthy enough to serve as soldiers. Salford did not endure AIDS, but it suffered especially badly from all the diseases of the day. The writer himself was struck by bouts of tuberculosis, a scourge well known in much of South Africa too.

One of the main reasons for ill health, as in poorer parts of South Africa today, was awful living conditions. The toilet, or privy, was always in a shack outside the main house. Homes were badly built and heated with coal fires that left a lung-choking smog in the air, not unlike the grey-brown cloud of coal smoke that creeps over Soweto and other townships in a South African winter. Security was a problem too: Britain in 1906 had roughly the same size prison population, 170 000 people, as South Africa today, at about 180 000 (though Britain's population of thirty-seven million was a little smaller than South Africa's forty-five million today). But the accounts of crime in Salford at the time – prostitution, failure to pay small fines, 'sleeping out' – pale into insignificance compared with the rates of violence and murder considered average in modern Soweto.

As I sat reading, I reflected that I have been to Manchester a few times; I've been to Salford too. I have even seen a play in a local theatre in Salford called *The Classic Slum*, where actors brought the same book to life. Salford today is still not the most beautiful part of Britain, nor of Manchester. It remains the less salubrious district of the greater city, a place with a long-established and deserved reputation for working-class hardship. But today Salford is no slum, not by any standard. Years of investment, growth and house-building, not unlike that going on in Soweto today, have made Salford a vastly cleaner, healthier and richer place. Many of the worst houses were bulldozed. In much of Britain the slum clearances of the last century led to vertical monsters, the inhuman towerblocks of the post-war years, that now seem little better. Nevertheless the slums went as the country grew, a welfare system was established, more jobs were created and better houses were built for ordinary people.

Sitting in the Johannesburg sunshine, an empty cup on my table, I thought about the writer of my book on the classic slum. He proudly said that the best descriptions of a place, and perhaps the best analyses, come from those who have grown up there, not from dewy-eyed historians – or journalists – who risk romanticising the past.

But here I claim a small exception to his rule. The writer of the book that I stumbled on in the Melville shop, was a man called Robert Roberts. He taught English in the great prison of Manchester, Strangeways, and didn't think of putting pen to paper to record his early life until near his death. He was my grandfather. I have no memory of sitting on his knee, a few months old, shortly before he died. So this book is one way that I can connect to him. By describing Salford in the early years of the last century my granddad shed a little light, for me, on South Africa's townships of today because there are striking similarities between the two places. There are big differences, of course – Salford had none of the political history of a Soweto; Soweto will be lucky to prosper as fast as Salford – but I choose to see what they have in common. For me, Soweto is a classic township.

Adam Roberts is the southern Africa correspondent of the *Economist* and has lived in Johannesburg for three years. He co-edited with Heidi Holland *From Jo'burg to Jozi: Stories about Africa's infamous city*, a collection of journalists' views of Johannesburg, published by Penguin in 2002. Robert Roberts published *The Classic Slum* in 1971, and later a second book on Salford, *A Ragged Schooling*.

North of the Limpopo

Simon Robinson

There is more than one Soweto in Africa. In Zambia stands a bazaar called Old Soweto Market that is filled with piles of discarded plastic bags, rotting bananas and tomatoes. Disease dances in the open sewers and children run barefoot among rickety wooden stalls, slime squelching between their toes. This festering sore became so putrid recently that fifty people died in a cholera outbreak. Realising that it finally had to do something after years of inaction, the Lusaka city council closed Soweto and promised to clean it up. Thank God, said the vendors, but where will we sell our wares in the meantime?

Further north, Uganda's Soweto is a poor suburb of the capital, Kampala. The area was originally a wetland and remains marshy and pungent to this day. Residents, who can't remember when their Soweto took its name, grow yams in their backyards and pay neighbours who are lucky enough to own a simple pit toilet a third of a rand, less than five

American cents, when they need to go.

The Soweto I know best, though, is in Kenya. This township, named for its South African cousin, is part of a sprawling Nairobi slum called Kibera. Unlike South Africa's Soweto, whose creation was very deliberate, Kibera is an accident. In the twenties a group of Sudanese soldiers – Nubians mostly – who had fought for Britain as part of the King's African Rifles, settled on a wooded slope south-west of the capital. Kenya's colonial masters left them alone but prevented any attempt to gain title to the land. But the Sudanese stayed anyway and built cheap houses which they rented to poor country folk lured to the city by the promise of jobs and fast money. Kibera exploded. At independence in 1963 the hill was dotted with trees. Today its slopes are covered by thousands of rusting tin shacks, home to more than a million people. There are thirteen villages in Kibera. Soweto is one of them.

The residents of Kenya's Soweto are proud of their neighbourhood. The dirt streets run with raw sewage and people regularly shit in plastic bags and then fling the 'flying toilets' out of their front doors. Rainstorms, common in Nairobi in April and November, wash away walls and even houses. Whole families sleep on the floor of a single room. Mothers cook over paraffin burners. Running water is a luxury. But there are also small joys: kids playing football, markets full of second-hand clothes, a fierce sense of community. Sowetans would rather live in one of Nairobi's tree-filled estates, of course. But disparage their surroundings and you will cop an earful. Threaten to evict them and they can turn violent. A few years ago Kenya's president criticised the Nubian slumlords for charging exorbitant rents. Emboldened, the residents of Kibera revolted. The Nubians, in turn, menaced anyone late with their rent. In the week-long fight that followed nine people were killed.

Just as in South Africa's Soweto, guns are common in

Nairobi's townships. The first time I ventured into Soweto I bought a gun. Sort of. The United Nations was meeting in New York to discuss the scourge of small arms around the world and I was late to the story. Many of my colleagues had visited northern Kenya where a flood of Kalashnikovs had turned local feuds into small scale wars. There was no time for me to travel and so, using an old journalistic conceit, I set out to show how easy it is to buy a gun in Africa.

A friend of a friend who had once lived in Soweto promised to introduce me to some 'businessmen'. Early one morning we made our way through a jumble of streets and alleyways that were designed by Soweto's residents, said my guide, to make it easier to escape chasing police. We arrived at a tiny two-roomed house. From under a bed holding a sleeping baby, a man dragged out a box filled with weapons. 'Most people rent,' he told me. 'It's cheaper.' A Kalashnikov costs seventy rand a day, about ten American dollars. Bullets cost between twelve and eighteen rand. You paid for what you used. As I left, having agreed to rent a submachine gun, a Kalashnikov and twenty bullets, all to be collected in a few days, he offered me the use of some of his men for 'any jobs' I might have. I declined and two days later, with the guns laid out in front of me, told him I no longer needed the weapons but that he could keep my deposit.

The strangest house in Kibera is a mansion that belongs to the former president. Actually, the house belongs to Kenya and was meant to be used as the vice-president's residence. But when President Daniel arap Moi took office in 1978 he stayed put in the house, preferring its cosier setting to the isolated and fancier State House. The house, known as Kabernet Gardens, is not actually in Kibera. It sits right on the edge of the slum; a last line of shacks nestles up beside its imposing brick wall. Over the years, Moi often invited his ministers to Kabernet Gardens to thrash out deals and set policies. A decision made there was rock. The president sometimes even hosted parties in his well-tended gardens. From there, standing on the freshly cut lawn of the slumlord to a nation, the good and the great had a front row view over the rolling waves of rusting tin and Kenya's pathetic decline.

Of course few people outside of Lusaka, Kampala and Nairobi know that there are other Sowetos. It's even possible to live in those cities and remain ignorant of their existence. There may be Sowetos in other parts of Africa too. Surely one of the murky inlets in Lagos is nicknamed for its southern doppelgänger? And was a part of Freetown dubbed Soweto during the worst fighting of the civil war? Maybe. The spread of the name is testament to the fact that Soweto is no longer merely a place but has become a byword for poverty and inequality. Africa is the world's Soweto. If Soweto, South Africa, can be reborn, Africans still have reason to hope.

Simon Robinson, *Time*'s Africa bureau chief, hails from Sydney, Australia. He lived in Nairobi, Kenya, for four years before moving to Johannesburg in 2002. He has reported from over twenty African countries including the Democratic Republic of Congo, Nigeria, Sierra Leone and Somalia. He spent much of 2003 in Iraq. He prefers Africa.

In the fifties

Anthony Sampson

In the fifties the south-west townships of Johannesburg –
which were only beginning to be called Soweto – were literally
off the map. The street-plans of the white suburbs were
extending ever further to the north, but they left huge blank
spaces to the south, between the mine dumps and the railway
lines: like early maps of Africa, they were uncharted areas for
the whites, terra incognita.

When I began visiting Soweto, once I became editor of
Drum magazine in 1951, I felt I was visiting another continent.
The bright lights disappeared; the tarred roads petered out
and turned into rocky tracks; the hillsides were covered with
endless vistas of tiny brick houses, shacks and breeze blocks.
There were no landmarks except the power station and giant
hoardings advertising cigarettes or soap which dwarfed the
houses below.

It was easy to get lost, and it was hard to tell one part of

Soweto from another: it seemed like a caricature of a socialist egalitarian society, with a proletariat of workers, all living in uniform box-houses, seething in the packed trains and buses, with no opportunity for individual expression, creativity or trade.

And as the apartheid government became more worried about political revolts Soweto was looking more like a military zone, designed to be patrolled and controlled by the police. That became clearer when the government, in 1955, began demolishing Sophiatown, the old multiracial slum much closer to the city centre, and moved its residents out to the new extension of Soweto called Meadowlands. The streets of Meadowlands were straight and symmetrical, dominated by the police station. In the event of organised resistance, the army and police in armoured cars could quickly enforce their own discipline.

But Soweto's appearance of sameness was totally misleading. It was full of contrasts and variety, a microcosm of black urban life: it included desperately poor families in shacks, but also some of the most remarkable leaders in all of Africa, who were to change the face of their country. As I got to know it better through my four years with *Drum*, I saw it not as a depersonalised settlement of identical box-houses, but as a cluster of close neighbourhoods, each with their own intimate relationships, street life and village atmosphere.

When I spent evenings in the Soweto shebeens, I was reminded of London pubs; when I stayed the night, I woke up to the sounds of children playing and dogs barking, which reminded me more of English villages of my youth than of the empty streets and isolated mansions of the white northern suburbs of Johannesburg.

It was Orlando, the relatively prosperous and long-established part of Soweto, which I got to know best, where so many of South Africa's future leaders and writers came from. The Mandelas and Sisulus were within walking distance,

215

and they were friends and neighbours of *Drum* writers including Henry Nxumalo, Todd Matshikiza and Es'kia Mphahlele.

In Orlando I came to feel myself at ease in a black world which I soon found much more stimulating and friendly than white Houghton or Yeoville, where I lived; and in Orlando I forged many friendships which lasted my lifetime. I was talking to Walter Sisulu in his Orlando home in 1953 when two Afrikaner policemen arrived to serve him with his banning notice. And it was in an Orlando church that I attended the christening of John Matshikiza, Todd's son, who was later to become an actor, poet and journalist, first in London, then in Johannesburg.

The intellectual life and vigour of Orlando reminded me of Bohemian London or undergraduate Oxford which I had left not long before. But Orlando could offer a much wider social life and experience: for its politicians and writers were compelled by the limitations of apartheid to be collectivists; to live cheek by jowl with quite other kinds of people, pressed together in trains, shebeens or social centres with entertainers, salesmen, messengers or gangsters.

The apartheid between blacks and whites had a contrary effect within the black communities: it diminished the class distinctions or social apartheid which bedevilled life in England, and gave black leaders a much greater opportunity to know their supporters and allies in their struggle.

And this concentration of activity and aspirations gave all of Soweto a dynamism and creativity which I found much more intense and exciting than the social world of white intellectuals and journalists, who might see themselves as Bohemians but were fearful of venturing into this alternative world. In fact it was not dangerous for whites to move in and out of Soweto: the apartheid police in the fifties were still relatively ineffective and amateurish. But only a few white communists, journalists or social rebels cared to cross the great divide between north and south.

It was the social taboo, the fear of miscegenation and of defiling racial purity, which kept the whites away from this parallel world, as much as the actual laws of apartheid, which was only a few years old. Eating and drinking with black people, let alone sexual intercourse, was seen as threatening the whole basis of white society.

It was when I was having dinner one evening in Soweto with Todd and Esme Matshikiza that I suddenly realised the ferocity of this taboo. Esme had served a wonderful meal in the tiny dining room, with sherry beforehand, followed by roast beef and Yorkshire pudding. We listened to African music, talked about writing books, when suddenly six black policemen appeared in the doorway, seized the sherry, searched the cupboards, and took Todd and a black friend off to the police station, where he had to pay a fine for possessing liquor.

I was escorted separately to the police station where after a long wait I was called in to see an Afrikaner sergeant. He seemed quite calm until he asked me why I was in Soweto. I explained I was having dinner with black friends. 'Eating with natives,' he exploded. 'How can you do it, man. Ag, it makes me sick, man.' He let me leave, with sheer disgust.

Anthony Sampson was the editor of *Drum* magazine for four years in the fifties. He now lives and works in London but makes regular trips to South Africa. He is the author of the authorised biography of Nelson Mandela, *Mandela*, and of several versions of *Anatomy of Britain*, the most recent, published in 2004, is entitled *Who Runs This Place*?

217

Of knives and cold showers

Diago Segola

Soweto. It is drab, lacks many facilities for a place of its size and its millions of inhabitants are largely poor, but somehow it's the place you'd much rather prefer to be. Why else do the ones that got away – that legion of former Sowetans who left the area for 'a better life' in the former so-called white suburbs – spend most of their leisure time in this vast, sprawling mix of houses, shacks and people that has over the years acquired an unsavoury reputation?

Go to any popular shebeen in Soweto on any weekday or better still over the weekend. And what do you find? Most of the émigrés are there, living it up as usual in a way they cannot do at their new places. They don't mind driving long distances every day from the northern, southern and other suburbs of Johannesburg to be where it's all happening.

It's the lure of Soweto.

If you are overseas, wherever you happen to be, two weeks

is long enough before your thoughts start drifting towards Soweto. Homesickness starts to creep in. Even the South Africans you meet abroad, like many of those who were in exile, will ask about Soweto rather than about the rest of the country. They miss it.

It's magnetic and swallows you up: you become an inseparable part of it. But for me it has not always been like that. Having grown up in Crown Mines, almost at the door of Johannesburg's city centre, I had always regarded Soweto as a backwater, some sort of Sodom or Gomorrah. Crown Mines, on the other hand, was the kind of place where every parent wished to raise his or her children – disciplined, almost crime-free, good sporting and other facilities, and churches of most denominations.

My first real taste of Soweto was during my high school days at The Rock – Orlando High School – from 1955. And I hated it. Not the school, but Soweto itself, or rather the crime in the place and the lifestyle of some of the youths there. It was the era when gangs were fashionable. And they plied their nefarious trade mostly at high schools.

The worst moments for Lizo, Benju, Philly and me were after school every day, when we walked with the young ladies who were our schoolmates and homegirls, down the main road through Mlamlankunzi to the bus stop in Noordgesig.

They would be waiting for us, that foul-mouthed, disrespectful group of delinquents at Lads Hostel, which was supposed to be a home for wayward boys. It was an almost daily ritual of being robbed of our few pennies for cigarettes, being sworn at and assaulted. One day one of them had an altercation with one of our female schoolmates. We thought it was the usual thing, but it turned out to be more serious. The thug drew a knife, charged at Stokie and stabbed her several times.

This happened on a glorious, sunny summer's day, not at night, along the main road running through Orlando, heavy

219

with traffic. Nobody intervened or lifted a finger. This painful incident reinforced my hatred for Soweto. I seriously thought about quitting school and severing all links with the infernal place. My mates and I started carrying knives ourselves, and we soldiered on with our schooling. Those were the days when getting home from work safely or anywhere else was something of an achievement in Soweto.

However, I stuck it out at Orlando High and slowly began to learn and realise that, in fact, there were more good people than baddies in Soweto. The picture of Soweto as a place riddled with crime no longer holds. True, you hear and read about some of the most horrific crimes committed there. But for a place of its size, poverty and other deprivations, Soweto is reasonably peaceful. You are more likely to be mugged and robbed in central Johannesburg and other parts of the city.

The beauty of Soweto lies in its people. They laugh, sing and joke despite life's hardships. Neighbours chat over fences and the teeming streets are meeting places.

One of the things I missed most when I first moved from Crown Mines to live in Orlando East, Soweto, were my daily showers – sometimes as many as three – with hot and cold water throughout the year. Baths and showers were a luxury for Soweto's millions of residents. The only place I knew then with a shower was the Orlando YMCA and I would walk more than a kilometre from my home to have a shower there.

I had just stepped into the refreshing hot water on a cold winter's day when a booming voice asked: 'Excuse me, are you a member?' The voice came from the late, amiable Mandla Dube (bless his soul), who was in charge of the place. 'No, I'm not a member,' I admitted. 'Then get out,' Mandla boomed back. He stood there as I dressed and made sure I was out of the water, and the place. Of course, Mandla was right. He ruled the Orlando Y with an iron hand. Why should he allow a non-member the use of its facilities, even if he knew that person? I later became a member and was able to have my showers. In true Soweto style, Mandla and I later laughed about the incident.

Or take the incident some years ago billed as 'Soweto's greatest day', when PW Botha visited the area, the first-ever visit by a white South African president. After a rather hurried tour of the place and a speech at Soweto's 'Parliament' in Jabulani, PW's entourage was hosted at a banquet at Diepkloof Hotel. It was an occasion of tight security – bodyguards and the security police – and all the media were barred. Lots to eat and drink was arranged for the media somewhere else in the hotel. The government top brass were all there – the likes of Pik Botha, Owen Horwood, Chris Heunis and other cabinet ministers – other government officials and members of the Soweto Urban Council.

I contrived, and succeeded, to make my way into the banquet. I had no seat and stood with the security police and the bodyguards against a wall as PW and his ministers addressed the councillors on 'important matters' imploring them not to leak anything to the press. Those leaders of Soweto – the Richard Maponyas, Tolika Makhayas and others – who we had vilified and maligned daily as sell-outs and puppets knew who I was and that I was a trespasser as I stood nervously in that banquet. I crossed my fingers, held my breath and looked down at the floor expecting that at any moment one of them would blow the whistle. There was no place to hide. But I need not have worried. I came out of the banquet unscathed.

As happened with Mandla Dube, we later laughed it off with some of those councillors. That is Soweto. There is that bond, that oneness among the people. They are one very large family. A new era has dawned for the people of Soweto since 1994. Their numbers have been swollen by hordes of new arrivals, mostly from Mozambique and Zimbabwe. Many of them are from the Horn of Africa: Eritrea, Ethiopia and Sudan. This was unthinkable in the not so distant past. Go to any of

Soweto's busiest areas such as the Baragwanath taxi rank and you are struck by the foreign dialects. The new arrivals compete for business at what was once the local traders' and hawkers' traditional, lucrative, turf.

But so far there has not been any word of animosities nor any fights. So-called xenophobia does not seem to exist among Soweto people. Three Sudanese men selling their wares from door to door in Orlando East said they were happy in the area and they had no problems with the people. That is the spirit of Soweto. Friendly and accommodating. To a large extent, the good overshadows the bad.

Diago Segola is a journalist on the daily newspaper *Sowetan*. Previously he worked for the South African Press Association (Sapa) and for the now defunct *Rand Daily Mail*.

Never again: the story of a beloved son

Charlene Smith

Sifiso means hope. He was Gladys' firstborn and, although mothers aren't supposed to have favourites, he was her beloved. In 1976 the Soweto uprising began close to their home in Central West Jabavu. Police and ambulance sirens wailed louder than mothers' tears. Teargas and smoke fogged the air. Students running before police bullets and sjamboks broke down the fence around the Oppenheimer Memorial Park in Central West Jabavu and stormed through its indigenous gardens. African sage and (the students believed) apartheid impimpi, Credo Mutwa, had already fled with three sangomas from the magical African village in its grounds.

Someone found turps, someone else found petrol, others had matches, and so students set alight one of the most important historical and cultural monuments in Soweto. But their act of anger has, perhaps, made it a more important monument, one filled with deeper meaning than the designer-built mausoleum of the Hector Petersen museum across the hill.

In those days young people threw their books out of school rucksacks which they stuffed with toiletries, a little food and clothes. They fled across borders to join, they hoped, an armed struggle against apartheid. Police and army convoys marked townships with the colours of bruises: blue, brown, yellow, their operational colours, brighter than the deep purple weals left on bodies. Gladys Mahlangu watched all of this and trembled. Sifiso was her love, her joy. Although a toddler, he could one day grow to be one of them, one of the stone throwers, one of the dead.

Sifiso's father was, like many South African fathers, no-where near his children. So Gladys sent messages to her mother in a village some one hundred kilometres from Pretoria in a barren, dirt bowl that would get Bantustan 'indepen-dence' a few years later. It would be known as KwaNdebele. Soon Sifiso's belongings were packed into a small suitcase and they left Soweto, moving past rock-strewn roads and burning vehicles, beyond police roadblocks and onto the quiet country roads of KwaNdebele where donkey carts and streams of people always seemed to be walking, walking, black ants among red dust flung by the occasional car.

Here Sifiso remained for close to seventeen years without returning to Soweto. When uprisings against the corrupt KwaNdebele Bantustan regime broke out, his mother and aunts spoke among themselves and decided it was still safer for a young, questioning boy than Soweto.

Sifiso would return to Soweto only when he was nineteen, as he waited to hear if his applications to a university or technikon had been successful. It was 1992, two years before freedom.

✳

224

I was in an office in the Munich Re building in downtown Johannesburg, interviewing Tokyo Sexwale and Chris Hani, when my beeper went off. The message said simply: '10 000 Zulu marching on Central West Jabavu'. I read it out loud; Chris said 'you'd better go'. It was the year before he would be assassinated; the year before pictures of Tokyo's weeping face would flash around the world.

I went to Kapitan's, an Indian restaurant a block away where Nelson Mandela and Oliver Tambo dined as young lawyers. Conflict always made me hungry, probably the effects of adrenaline, so I bought a half dozen samoosas. It was the year before Oliver Tambo died; two years before Nelson Mandela would become president.

On that day there was conflict too on the East Rand in Vosloorus and KwaThema; there were clashes in KwaZulu-Natal; Sebokeng and Evaton were restless. So I was the only journalist to arrive in Central West Jabavu.

I drove through rock-strewn roads and burning barricades. I stood in a park on a hill looking down into Central West Jabavu; I was across from the Oppenheimer Memorial. There was the regular report of rifle and handgun fire as well as isolated grenade explosions. A house was burning. An impi of Zulu hostel residents on the hillocks of the Oppenheimer Memorial were shielding behind bushes and boulders as they fired on the residents of CWJ. The residents returned with rocks and swearing; occasional reports from their ranks suggested at least one person had a handgun.

I began driving down a boulder-strewn road towards the residents. As I did I saw a young man stagger towards a fence and lean over it, another young man ran up behind him, put his arms around and lifted him.

'My God,' I thought, 'this looks just like the Hector Petersen picture.' I yelled, 'Bring him here, bring him here, put him in the car.' The young Comrade was staggering under his friend's weight but ran surprisingly fast and slid into the back seat.

225

'You,' I grabbed another young man by the sleeve, 'get into the front seat.' He obeyed without question as I took off my jacket and stuffed it into the blood pouring from Sifiso's abdomen. 'Don't let him fall asleep, keep talking to him, keep talking,' I told his friend.

'And you,' I instructed the other Comrade, 'hang out the window and tell them to clear the tyres and the rocks.' He did, hastening our progress through streets littered with burning barricades. 'Thank you, thank you,' I muttered in between swearing at those who didn't move rocks fast enough.

I prayed silently but out loud tried to be reassuring, 'not much longer, not much longer, speak to him, speak to him, don't let him sleep'.

I screeched into the casualty area at Lesedi Clinic shouting 'Get a stretcher, a stretcher, a young man has been shot.' They took Sifiso from the Comrade's arms and into a closed room. We slid onto the floor, our backs against the wall, silent. A few minutes later a door opened and a young doctor said, 'Who is his relative?' We looked at each other. 'We don't know,' I finally said. The doctor answered, 'I'm afraid he is dead.' A nurse had already put my blood-soaked jacket into a blue plastic bag.

Nothing seemed real. We stood there, uncertain, and then I said to the two young Comrades, 'I'll take you back.' We stopped at a cafe for Cokes, our mouths were unnaturally dry. 'Does anyone know his mother,' I asked. One boy did. 'You need to tell her,' I said. He shook his head, the other boy did too. 'I can't,' I said. 'I'm a journalist, I don't know her . . .' But I knew I would have to. It's the worst thing I've ever had to do.

There was still fighting in CWJ when we got back, Sifiso's home was less than a block from the main clashes. The boys showed me where it was and vanished. I parked outside and knocked on the door, my heart pounding. 'I need to speak to Sifiso's mother,' I said; my mouth was dry and I felt dizzy.

226

I was led through a cool room with brown chairs grouped against white walls, an upmarket shebeen. I paused briefly before going into a large bedroom. She was talking on the phone, a young boy of about thirteen was sitting on the edge of the bed closest to the door, looking down. He had the saddest face in the world. He knew. There were other people in the room but I don't remember them, in my memory they formed a silent frame. Gladys' eyes and mine locked, I didn't want to say what I had to. She asked, 'Are you MK?'

'No,' I said. 'I'm very sorry but Sifiso is dead.'

She said she wanted to see his body and I took her. As we got outside a bakkie of plain clothes cops had arrived; they were armed with rifles and laughed and joked as if they were part of a hunting party, which is probably what they were. I swallowed my rage and helped Gladys into the car.

Sifiso had already been transferred to the mortuary. She wanted to be alone with him, thank God, and I waited in the concrete courtyard outside. Then I took her back home and made her sweet tea; she wouldn't let go of my hand. Sifiso, she said, had been home only two weeks. 'All those years I tried to protect him,' she sobbed.

Back at the *Sunday Times* I parked the company car and the drivers came up to me. 'Charlene,' one of the indunas said, putting his arm around me, 'are you all right, you look terrible? You look like you have seen a ghost.' My face was devoid of colour, my hands shook and I stammered when I spoke. I'd seen hundreds of people die before, but he was the first person to die in my car, in a sense the first person whose life I'd felt responsible for saving and the first person whose relatives I had to tell. The shot that killed him wounded me; eleven years later I can't write about him without crying.

※

I'd learnt an important lesson as a young journalist a decade

227

before. A few hours after a raid in Maseru, Lesotho, a young African National Congress comrade, Oupa, showed me around the killing fields of the South African Defence Force. Soldiers had murdered forty-nine ANC members and Lesotho nationals, including children. In one small house SADF gunfire had exploded two gas canisters ripping apart the bodies of a man, his wife and two children aged two and four. A woman was sweeping the remains of their bodies. I felt my knees buckling and a wail building in my belly. I looked at Oupa: he was nineteen, these were his friends, he showed no emotion, he was doing his duty to them. And so I did my duty to Sifiso and his mother, I pushed my emotions back, wrote the story and went home and cried.

I had promised Gladys I would check on her the next day, a Saturday. Early that morning I drove back to Soweto. She was sleeping a tranquillised sleep. However I was asked to go to another house up the road. This was nearer the conflict of the day before, directly opposite a railway line embankment that hid the hostel where the previous day's attackers had been.

Here, too, a young man had died, and his mother and aunts sat in a darkened room, blankets around their shoulders, their legs straight ahead of them, a small candle flickering. The family showed me windows broken by attackers the previous day. Then they sat me at the kitchen table. Someone fetched a shoe box, opened it, and rolled a grenade onto the table.

'This came in through a window yesterday and landed in the lounge, what should we do with it?'

The pin was intact. My mind whirled, I abhor weapons and can't touch them. I was too frightened to take it in my car, and if I did, where would I take it to? Calling the police was out of the question because they would terrorise the residents and conduct a house to house search. If we buried it in the garden someone might one day dig it up and blow himself up. We couldn't just throw it into the nearby river because a child might find it.

There was no option but to pull the pin, but none of us had any expertise. I phoned a lawyer I'd worked with at the Independent Board of Informal Inquiry into Repression, the first body to investigate and confirm death squad activity. I'd helped set it up and worked on the first investigations. I hadn't been perturbed by phone and mail intercepts or even about being followed, but after my Labrador kept someone up a tree for most of one night I quit. A young lawyer who came onto the team was later blown up by a set of headphones sent by security police.

I called one of the lawyers and asked what I should do about the grenade. He suggested I call a prominent forensic scientist, who agreed to come out. He photographed the grenade, identified it and told me to take it to the police. I refused. He said he would phone them to fetch it. I told him if he did they would terrorise the community.

As we argued we could hear the terrifying sound of an impi moving toward us, with their low deep *Usuthu* chant. I lost my temper. 'Do you hear that sound? That's an impi on the march, if we don't blow that grenade soon, they'll be here. I'm not sticking around for them. If you don't dispose of it now, I'm going to leave you here.'

He looked at me as if I'd taken leave of my senses. 'You wouldn't.'

I picked up my car keys, 'Has no one told you I'm crazy?'

He pulled the pin.

In the year that followed, Sifiso's younger brother joined a group of comrades and disappeared. His mother's home was burnt down, no one knows by whom. We stayed in contact and she gave me a video of Sifiso's funeral. I had neither the courage to attend his funeral nor to watch the video. We spoke long and often. I think that she felt that as I was one of the last people with him when he died, in some way I carried part of his spirit with me. Her nerves deteriorated, even though she worked as a nurse. There was pathetically little psychological help for her, and none was ever offered to Sifiso's younger brother. In two years she had three nervous breakdowns. She gave up her job and moved to her family village in KwaNdebele. I'm ashamed to say, I lost touch.

Charlene Smith has written six books, including *Robben Island* (Struik), *Proud of Me: Speaking Out Against Sexual Violence and HIV* (Penguin) and *Patricia de Lille* (Spearhead). She works as a writer, consultant and documentary film maker. A winner of several awards, she has worked for the *Sunday Times*, the *Star*, SAFM, *Financial Mail* and others, and has written as a freelancer for foreign publications including the *Los Angeles Times*. Some names have been changed in this story.

Windows wide shut

Christina Stucky

My white South African hosts picked me up at the Rotunda bus station in downtown Johannesburg on a hot day in late February. It had been a disorienting month. South Africa with its jarring array of contrasts seemed both disturbingly familiar and comfortingly strange. We drove through the city centre as though crossing a war zone. Despite the heat, I was instructed to lock the doors and keep the windows shut. Johannesburg's Central Business District, said my hosts, was full of jewellery snatchers and car hijackers. As we made our way along its crowded streets, I watched through the rolled-up windows as the city went about its usual, unthreatening business.

My hosts graciously welcomed me into their northern suburbs home. They took me to parties and dinners where people called 'Pips' and 'Johnny' spoke of rugby and cricket, shared the latest crime stories and related details of recent holidays to Thailand and Europe. In the background, like ghosts, the black staff cooked, cleaned, and ironed. With remarkable regularity I was told how loved and 'part of the family' the black staff was. It seemed important to white South Africans to assure foreigners of this unique bond.

A lot felt strange during those weeks. The first democratic elections I had come to witness, and Soweto, South Africa's most famous township I was eager to visit, seemed to be part of another world. No one I met in those first few weeks in South Africa had been to a township, few had even been to downtown Johannesburg. Their heads were as filled as mine with the images of dusty township streets, burning tyres and hostile, fist-waving crowds that I had seen on television in Europe. Everyone I met at those parties in Johannesburg's north told me that Soweto was too dangerous for whites.

Shortly after my arrival, about six weeks before the country's first democratic elections, I began working at *The Star* newspaper. There attitudes to Soweto were different. Going to a township was *de rigueur*. Yet many white South African journalists spoke of 'covering townships' the way European or American correspondents speak of covering a war in a foreign land – with bravado, a hint of fear and a lot of distance. These journalists talked over 'going into' the townships as a European journalist might speak of travelling to Liberia to cover a war. Of course for many black journalists 'going into the townships' was a daily ritual. It meant going home.

My first chance to visit Soweto came on March 17, 1994. I was sent to cover President FW de Klerk's seven-stop election roadshow which included speeches and lunch in Soweto. It would be a historic moment: the first National Party rally in Soweto addressed by an NP leader.

My first glimpse of Soweto from the air-conditioned media bus was a blur of beige and brown. Matchbox houses flew past the window along with dusty shrubs, walls daubed with graffiti, plastic bags floating like jellyfish, billowing dust. There was a noticeable lack of trees. But there were no burning tyres and the small crowds gathering around De Klerk were not hostile. When our convoy of buses and cars entered Soweto children waved, pointed their fingers like guns or stared at the mass of white faces driving past.

In Mofolo North De Klerk emerged from his car and squeezed past market stalls and chicken cages in search of black hands to shake. He told shoppers that they needed more space and promised to see to it. He disappeared as quickly as he came. At lunch the convoy pulled in at the Ernest Oppenheimer Hall in Meadowlands. His stop lasted long enough for some food and more shaking of hands. Then he was swept away to the next destination on his schedule. And I got left behind.

My handbag, colleagues and the rest of the roadshow moved on to the next stop, while I, notebook and pen in hand, felt a slow rise of panic. I asked a South African photographer for a lift. He said the car was full. 'What are you going to do?' he added with a challenging smirk. I asked the NP media man. Bending over his plate of food, he gruffly told me that he was in charge of the media until lunch. I was, therefore, no longer his responsibility.

I had no idea where I was or where the roadshow was heading. I was annoyed with the photographer and the NP man. Bastards, I hissed angrily. How was I going to get out of Soweto? After two weeks of sitting in the newsroom covering stories I could have written anywhere, I was not about to give the news editor a reason never to send me to a township again. I braced myself and made the rounds among the National Party membership.

Finally, I found an NP man who took pity on a white foreign woman adrift in a black township. In his kind, patronising way he took my arm and handed me to a black NP councillor from Soweto. The request to drive me to the next stop sounded more like an instruction. With obvious reluctance the councillor agreed.

His grey suit shone like fish scales in the late summer sun. Sweat ran in rivulets from his head and slipped down his collar. The man was polite but spoke little, clearly uncomfortable with this scenario: a black National Party councillor driving a white woman through Soweto. Once in the car, a familiar ritual unfolded. He leaned across me to lock my door and instructed me to keep the windows shut, despite the heat. Soweto, he said, was full of *tsotsis*, ready to rob him of his car and me of my virtue. Through the rolled-up car windows I watched Soweto go about its usual, unthreatening business, while the man drove as fast as he could out of the township.

Christina Stucky arrived in South Africa from Switzerland in 1994. Since then she has lived in Johannesburg, working as a local reporter, editor, media trainer and as a foreign journalist. She was the chairperson of the Johannesburg Foreign Correspondents' Association until early 2004.

Getting a new perspective

Nicholas Williamson

In 1996 Soweto crashed into my consciousness as nothing ever had before and left me changed in a way that I am still working through.

Like most *koloniste* citizens of my city I had been aware of Soweto as a place that existed on the south-west side of town, but like that other region now called Ekurhuleni, to the south-east of our city, it was a non-place where one never went. As a *mlungu*, or *larney*, a *koloniste*, I had no reason to go there. I knew no one there and had no business there. For most of my life I had no right to a permit to visit Soweto or any other dumping ground for dispossessed people in the country.

Not only that, but until I was twenty I had spoken to perhaps no more than a dozen dispossessed people, so completely were they pushed aside from my awareness. Soweto was a non-place for me. There were no road signs to denote it existed. When I eventually did go there, regularly on business in the late eighties, I found no road signs inside it either. It was a vast alienated no-place, with uncounted millions living in zones suggested by abstract numbers still meaningless to me. In his most glorious moments Nietzsche could not have found a metaphor to describe such a wasteland. Even its name was an imposed acronym.

My business was supplying specialised roofs that had to be built off site and trucked in with armed guards. Without the armed guards the trucks would otherwise be stoned and burned. I felt Soweto was on the move: a sleeping giant awakening and brimming with a vitality and a directness that I had never encountered before.

But that business failed, finished off by the uncertainty of the early nineties. I had been driven to the wall. My ailing firm staggered to an end. Eventually to survive I took a job as a secondary school substitute teacher; to keep sane I started writing prose and was struggling to find a voice.

The day came when I found myself in a classroom owned by The Sowetans, as they proudly termed themselves. This was the day Soweto crashed into my consciousness. There were forty-eight 16-year-olds crammed into a room built for twenty. They were fresh from the barricades and spoiling for a fight, especially with someone they saw as a former oppressor.

I was handed a pile of books to use with the class. There was a collection of South African short stories, and I barely had time to scan the contents and find one to study before a storm erupted. I chose Herman Charles Bosman and asked someone to begin an oral reading. We hadn't covered more than a page when the worst of words, the K-word, Kaffir, appeared in print and someone read it, incredulously; realising what it was as he spoke it, and as if on some pre-designated cue, forty-eight healthy young humans erupted into chaos.

I had been shot four times the year before in a neighbourhood gunfight, and was still in a deeply traumatised state. I was nowhere near the exit. Chairs flew and tables were overturned. Rage poured about the room. I didn't know what to do, so I did nothing but wait for the uproar to become simply tension.

Then they asked the inevitable question. Why the word? Why the pointed nature of the word? I had standard answers, related to context, historical perspective and other denialist stuff. But I didn't think it was helpful to piss them off with such evasions. So I told them 'That's how it was.'

'But why does the writer not tell us that the other people in the story are *mlungus*?' a voice asked. 'Why must he tell us that these people, in this part, are us, dispossessed people, but we just have to know that everyone else is probably a *larney*.' I said nothing. He persisted. 'Why?'

I said nothing because I didn't know the answer. The tension grew, until it seemed the place was about to explode again. Another scornful voice broke in. 'Aah, it's because the writer thinks only *larneys* read.' They looked at me, waiting for a response. Then, as if a light had been switched on, I realised she was right.

'Yes,' I said.

Nicholas Williamson is a poet, writer and bloggist (an online-publisher who frequently adds to a personal website of his own writings). His novels *The Buffalo Hunters* and *The Ashanti Raider*, plus his poetry collection *The random notes of a marginalised man* are published on his web page www.Williamsonreport.co.za

Acknowledgements

This book grew very fast, and is only possible thanks to the enormous help of many different people. Heidi Holland pointed out that 2004 marks a century for Soweto and she first suggested the idea for the book. Her prodding and chasing of authors was also essential. She and Anne Hammerstad made sure we tracked down Sam Nhlengethwa for the excellent cover image. Moeletsi Mbeki brought Joe Thloloe into the project from the very beginning. Milton Nkosi and Ofeibea Quist-Arcton, whose offices are within easy nagging distance of mine, were the toughies who helped to recruit several writers and forced them to stick to cruel deadlines.

Adam Roberts

Further reading

Berry, Abe. *Johannesburg in Drawings and Text*. Tafelberg publishers 1982.

Bonner, Phil and Lauren Segal. *Soweto: A History*. Maskew Miller Longman 1998.

Holland, Heidi and Adam Roberts. *From Jo'burg to Jozi: Stories about Africa's infamous city*. Penguin Books 2002.

Holland, Heidi. *Born in Soweto*. Penguin Books 1994.

Huddleston, Trevor. *Naught for Your Comfort*. London: Collins 1956.

MacMillan, W M. *Africa Emergent*. Pelican Books 1938,1949.

Magubane, Peter and Charlene Smith. *Soweto*. Struik publishers 2001.

Mandy, Nigel. *A City Divided; Johannesburg and Soweto*. Macmillan South Africa 1984.

Mphahlele, Es'kia. *Down Second Avenue*. Faber 1971.

Musiker, Naomi and Reuben. *A Concise Historical Dictionary of Greater Johannesburg*. Francolin Publishers 2000.

O'Rourke, P J. *Holidays in Hell*. Picador 1988.

Palestrant, Ellen. *Johannesburg One Hundred*. AD Donker 1986.

Roberts, Robert. *The Classic Slum: Salford Life in the First Quarter of the Century*. Penguin Books 1971.

Thompson, Leonard. *A History of South Africa*. Yale Nota Bene 2001.